Teaching Graphic Novels in the English Classroom

Alissa Burger
Editor

Teaching Graphic Novels in the English Classroom

Pedagogical Possibilities of Multimodal Literacy
Engagement

Editor
Alissa Burger
Department of English
Culver Stockton College
Canton, Missouri
USA

ISBN 978-3-319-87562-0   ISBN 978-3-319-63459-3   (eBook)
DOI 10.1007/978-3-319-63459-3

This Palgrave Macmillan imprint is published by Springer Nature
The registered company is Springer International Publishing AG
The registered company address is: Gewerbestrasse 11, 6330 Cham, Switzerland

CONTENTS

CHAPTER 1

Introduction

Alissa Burger

In recent years, graphic novels have been making their way into a wide variety of classrooms, from elementary schools to college courses and libraries, to teach not just classic and contemporary literature, but also memoir, history, science, and more, joining the conversation in almost every discipline. As Robert G. Weiner and Carrye Kay Syma argue in *Graphic Novels and Comics in the Classroom: Essays on the Educational Power of Sequential Art*, "In the past 10 to 15 years, the use of sequential art in education has exploded. Teachers in secondary and elementary schools, professors in universities, and instructors of all kinds are using comics and graphic novels to illustrate points about gender, history, sociology, philosophy, mathematics, and even medicine. It is no longer a question of whether sequential art should be used in educational settings, but rather how to use it and for what purpose" (1).

There are numerous benefits to teaching graphic novels, including engaging reluctant readers, encouraging students to view familiar material from a new perspective, and critically engaging students' multiple literacies. James Bucky Carter explains that "A substantial, expanding body of evidence asserts that using graphic novels and comics in the classroom produces effective learning opportunities over a wide range of subjects and

A. Burger (✉)
Department of English, Culver-Stockton College, Canton, MO, USA

A. Burger (ed.), *Teaching Graphic Novels in the English Classroom*,
DOI 10.1007/978-3-319-63459-3_1

benefits various student populations, from hesitant readers to gifted students" (1).

In particular, reading comics and graphic novels helps students develop multimodal literacy skills, through the complex combination of image and text. As Lynell Burmark argues, "the primary literacy of the twenty-first century is visual .... Our students must learn to process both words and pictures. To be visually literate, they must learn to 'read' (consume/interpret) and 'write' (produce/use) visually rich communications. They must be able to move gracefully and fluently between text and images, between literal and figurative worlds" (5) and Weiner and Syma also underscore this importance: "The combination of images with text in order for students to understand and interpret the world is probably the most important aspect of teaching literacy in the 21st century" (5). In *Comics as History, Comics as Literature: Roles of the Comic Book in Scholarship, Society, and Entertainment*, Annessa Ann Babic draws on the work of Joseph Witek and his argument that "comics are designed with highly developed narratives, grammar, and vocabulary based on an inextricable combination of verbal and visual elements" (5). Graphic novels are an excellent tool for developing these interrelated skills and preparing students to critically engage with and respond to a world that requires simultaneous and interactive multiple literacies. When reading a graphic narrative, the reader has to not only parse the literal meaning of the written and visual text on the page, but also critically consider the ways in which both mediums work together, situated within the unique format of the graphic novel as a whole, employing a complex wealth of terminology to describe what they see, what it means, and their own critical response to the text.[1] As Weiner and Syma argue, in reading these graphic novels, "students are using a format that provides an opportunity for active engagement. Their minds are lively when reading comics. The readers involve their minds with both the visual and narrative content, hopefully resulting in great comprehension and interest" (5), both through textual understanding and critical response. Our contemporary culture is one of dynamic multimodal and interactive texts, a trend which extends well beyond the classroom, and for which graphic novel reading will serve our students well. For instance, the vast majority of websites include text and image, as well as advertisements, links to related stories or materials, or embedded video or audio materials, combinations which create a range of ways in which we can interact with the text before us, actively negotiating and choosing elements on which to focus rather than having a passive reading experience.

A question that is often raised when considering the inclusion of graphic novels in the classroom is whether or not graphic novels count as "literature." In addition to the benefits of textual complexity and active reader engagement, graphic novels demonstrate the same characteristics as more traditional works in the same genre. For example, a memoir shares the life experiences of its author, regardless of the medium in which it is presented, while fictional graphic novels possess the same literary elements as a short story or novel, such as plot, setting, characterization, and point of view, even if those elements are realized or depicted through the combination of text and image rather than text alone, as in their more traditional counterparts. Beyond definition and core elements, there is debate about what counts as "literary," a concept that polices the boundaries of canonical literature. Merriam-Webster defines literature, in part, as "writings in prose or verse; *especially*: writings having excellence of form or expression and expressing ideas of permanent or universal interest" (emphasis original). This definition points toward the age-old debate of what counts as canonical and worthy of study, a benchmark of which many critics argue graphic novels fall short. However, if we consider a definition of literature that considers a work's effect on the reader, whether that means drawing them into a compelling story or immersing them in a perspective far different from their own, it is clear that graphic novels succeed at that level of engagement, evidenced by readers' interest, excitement, and positive responses to these kinds of stories, both inside and outside the classroom. In addition, this definition, which demands a direct correlation of literary and textual, elides the multimodal complexity of 21st-century storytelling, where stories can include images as well as words and where tales are told in online and social media spaces as well as on the page, like Jennifer Egan's story "Black Box," which the writer delivered through a series of tweets.[2] Finally, the debate as to whether or not graphic novels count as literature can also be useful in framing the pedagogical discussion, as we ask students to consider, respond to, and perhaps even make an argument for the questioning, challenging, and creation of the canon, posing, as one contributor to this collection suggests, the canon creation debate as an active and contested discussion to which students can contribute their own voices and opinions.

Graphic narratives in their myriad forms have great potential for incorporation in the English classroom, from introductory and advanced writing courses to creative writing, literature surveys, and upper-level literature seminars. We can introduce students to complex rhetorical concepts and terminology with *Understanding Rhetoric: A Graphic Guide to Writing* by

Elizabeth Losh, Jonathan Alexander, Kevin Cannon, and Zander Cannon, a unique format that not only makes these often challenging ideas more accessible to students, but also serves as an ideal springboard in helping them design multimedia assignments of their own, combining text, image, and other mediums. There is a wide range of memoirs, including Art Spiegelman's Pulitzer Prize-winning *Maus*, Marjane Satrapi's *Persepolis*, and Alison Bechdel's *Fun Home*, which can provide students a glimpse into places, lives, and experiences much different than their own, creating connection and empathy. There are countless adaptations of classic literature, from graphic novel versions of many of Shakespeare's plays to more creative reimaginings or reinventions, like Alan Moore's *The League of Extraordinary Gentlemen*, a critical engagement of a range of Victorian literary figures and influences. Many of these graphic novels also present opportunities for further interdisciplinary engagement, as several of them have been adapted into films as well, positioning the graphic novel as one part of a larger conversation, drawing on classical literary traditions and dynamically influencing contemporary popular culture.

The chapters in this collection present a wide range of experiences and opportunities for incorporating graphic narratives and novels into the English classroom, sharing concrete, specific examples and pedagogies, as well as raising questions and proposing possibilities for new approaches. The authors have incorporated graphic novels into a wide variety of classes, from introductory Freshman Composition to intermediary writing and Honors courses, as a foundation for research and an inspiration for creative writing, in literature survey courses and in upper-level literature seminars. However, each of these essays is built upon one shared core belief: that in the combination of text and image, graphic narratives provide our students with a unique, dynamic opportunity for reading, learning, and engagement that cannot be achieved through text or image alone.

This collection is divided into three sections. The first focuses on different possibilities for incorporating graphic novels into the composition classroom, from introductory to advanced writing. In his chapter on "Not Just Novels: The Pedagogical Possibilities of the Graphic Narrative," Andrew Bourelle discusses his approach of introducing students to a wide range of shorter graphic narratives over the course of the semester, rather than just a few full-length graphic novels, which gives them the opportunity to see, engage with, and respond to a variety of different styles and approaches, highlighting the breadth and depth of the medium in a way that isn't possible through a handful of representative, longer examples.

Understanding Rhetoric: A Graphic Guide to Writing has quickly become a staple in college writing classrooms since its publication in 2014, and it is one of the central works utilized and discussed in Sara Austin's "*Understanding Rhetoric,* Understanding Genre: A Rhetorical Genre Studies Approached Writing Course," where she develops and discusses an intermediary writing studies course in which students explore, critically engage with, and write within a genre of their choice. Riki Thompson's "Writing through Comics" is the final chapter in this section, in which she discusses a comics-writing approach within the creative writing classroom, guiding students through thinking critically about the balance and interaction of text and image, character development, and world building, among a wealth of other creatively-focused writing activities that culminate in the students producing and distributing their own comics. Each of the chapters in this section provides detailed descriptions of specific assignments, many of which could be easily incorporated into writing classes at a variety of levels to aid students in meaningfully engaging with text, image, and the connections between the two, as well as exploring the different forms their own writerly voice can take.

The second section foregrounds graphic novels as a unique literary genre, well-deserving of inclusion and incorporation into the literature classroom. While the question of the literary merit of comics and graphic novels underscores many discussions of their use within the English classroom, the authors in this section advocate for graphic novels to be considered as literature in their own right, and highlight the various classroom settings and connections where they have found them to promote productive discussions and active learning, from survey courses to upper-level seminars. Lauren Perry's "Teaching the History and Theory of American Comics: 20th-Century Graphic Novels as a Complex Literary Genre" not only argues that comics should be considered literary, but that they are complex, nuanced, and in many ways even more challenging than traditional literature, a value underscored in her approach to comics from both historical and literary perspectives as she introduces students to the background, development of, and discourse surrounding the medium, as well as a wide range of comics themselves. Alison Halsall presents several opportunities for including the graphic novel in college English courses in her chapter "'What Is the Use of a Book ... Without Pictures or Conversations?': Incorporating the Graphic Novel into the University Curriculum," with extended examples including using Frank Miller's *300* to discuss the epic genre and reading Alan Moore's *The League of Extraordinary Gentlemen* through its engagement with Victorian culture and literary conventions, highlighting the ways in which these readings deepen students' understandings of both the graphic novel format and the conventions of the more traditionally "literary." Guy Risko's "'Does Doctor Manhattan Think?': Alan Moore's *The Watchmen* and a 'Great Books' Curriculum in the Early College Setting" shifts the focus a bit, exploring the incorporation of Moore's text into a humanistic seminar with a strong basis in historical and philosophical discourse, designed to orient upper-level high school students to a college experience through a dual-credit approach; as a result, Risko explores the question of how *Watchmen* can be brought into conversation with more canonical literature and philosophical debate, while also considering the ways in which professors can engage high school students within the early college paradigm. The concluding chapter in this section is Allison Powell's "'If He Be Mr. Hyde, We Shall Be Mr. See': Using Graphic Novels, Comic Books, and the Visual Narrative in the Gothic Literature Classroom," which focuses on a genre-specific, upper-level seminar course, in this case exploring the ways in which graphic narratives can be used to help students understand and engage with the often textually and thematically dense literature of the Gothic tradition, using the example of Robert Louis Stevenson's *Strange Case of Dr. Jekyll and Mr. Hyde*—among others—to show how introducing the visual narrative to the Gothic literature classroom not only bridges gaps for less advanced learners but engages all levels of students, better ensuring mastery of complex Gothic topics. As these literature course-based examples show, there is a wide range of opportunities for including graphic novels within literature courses, whether in the integration of a single visual narrative within a largely traditional literature class or in a course that foregrounds the literary nature of the graphic novel format, building a curriculum entirely around these types of texts.

The third and final section explores the potential for graphic novels to spark discussions of social justice, identity, and empathy with our students. Literature is immensely powerful in creating opportunities for the reader to take a look into someone else's life and gain insight into another's experiences, engagement that often works to create connection and empathy with the struggles of others, and each of the essays in this section highlights the ways in which graphic novels can be used to create understanding, empathy, and social awareness that can engage students in the fight for social justice, whether in their own communities or around the world. Susanna Hoeness-Krupsaw's chapter, "Teaching *March* in the Borderlands between Social Justice and Pop Culture," focuses on John Lewis's three-volume graphic novel memoir, which connects students to the historic Civil Rights movement, Lewis's personal experiences and resultant activism, and the links between past fights for racial equality and contemporary issues of racism, discrimination, and violence. Jennifer Phillips analyzes representations of refugees and the Global Migration Crisis, particularly in discourse surrounding refugees in Australia, with her chapter "Revising the Rhetoric of 'Boat People' through the Interactive Graphic Adaptation of Nam Le's 'The Boat,'" highlighting the ways in which the unique interactive format of the online adaptation immerses readers not just visually, but also through sound, movement, and active engagement as they scroll their way through the narrative, this new experience allowing them to see a familiar story from a fresh and powerful perspective, with a level of empathy and engagement that has the potential to overcome the statistical numbing many students, readers, and citizens face today. Finally, William Cordeiro and Season Ellison co-write "Performative Texts and the Pedagogical Theatre: Alison Bechdel's *Fun Home* as Compositional Model," in which they frame reading, learning, teaching, and writing as acts of performance and invite students to engage in a variety of identity exercises that encourage self-reflection and empathy, as they discuss incorporations of Bechdel's graphic novel that could be adapted or put to use in a variety of writing courses, from introductory writing to Honors-level seminars. As each of these authors notes, reading a narrative has been proven more effective in eliciting empathy than a recitation of statistics, and the addition of a visual component can significantly increase this impact, making graphic novels an ideal fit for encouraging students to consider perspectives other than their own, gain insight into the world around them, respond with empathy, and increase their capacity for social understanding, moving toward activism and social justice.

The essays featured in this collection provide specific examples and detailed assignment overviews that can be easily implemented, but it is our hope that they also serve as a point of departure for a larger conversation, encouraging readers to move toward innumerable other possibilities for incorporating graphic novels within the English classroom, creating a wide range of pedagogical possibilities for multimodal engagement.

Notes

1. *GetGraphic.org*'s "Some Graphic Novel Basics" provides a quick and accessible overview of reading strategies and basic terminology, suitable for

beginning graphic novel readers, while Scott McCloud's classic *Understanding Comics* is the gold standard for a detailed and comprehensive introduction to the medium.

2. Egan's story can be read in its entirety on the *New Yorker*'s website at http://www.newyorker.com/magazine/2012/06/04/black-box-2

WORKS CITED

Babic, Annessa Ann. "Introduction." *Comics as History, Comics as Literature: Roles of the Comic Book in Scholarship, Society, and Entertainment*, edited by Annessa Ann Babic, Fairleigh Dickinson UP, 2014, pp. 1–14.

Burmark, Lynell. "Visual Literacy: What You Get Is What You See." *Teaching Visual Literacy: Using Comic Books, Graphic Novels, Anime, Cartoons, And More to Develop Comprehension and Thinking Skills*, edited by Nancy Frey and Douglas Fisher, Corwin, 2008, pp. 5–25.

Carter, James Bucky. "Introduction—Carving a Niche: Graphic Novels in the English Language Arts Classroom." *Building Literacy Connections with Graphic Novels*, edited by James Bucky Carter, National Council of Teachers of English, 2007, pp. 1–25.

Egan, Jennifer. "Black Box." *The New Yorker*, 4 June and 11 June 2012, http://www.newyorker.com/magazine/2012/06/04/black-box-2

"Literature." MerriamWebster.com, 2017. https://www.merriam-webster.com/dictionary/literature

McCloud, Scott. *Understanding Comics*. William Morrow, 1994. "Some Graphic Novel Basics." *GetGraphic.org*, 2007, http://www.getgraphic.org/resources/HowtoReadaGraphicNovel.pdf

Weiner, Robert G. and Carrye Kay Syma. "Introduction." *Graphic Novels and Comics in the Classroom: Essays on the Educational Power of Sequential Art,* edited by Robert G. Weiner and Carrye Kay Syma, McFarland, 2013, pp. 1–10.

PART I

Reading, Writing, and Graphic Narratives

CHAPTER 2

Not Just Novels: The Pedagogical Possibilities of the Graphic Narrative

Andrew Bourelle

Recently, I was teaching an advanced composition class where I made an interesting discovery. The class was themed and focused on comic books and graphic novels, using the genre of sequential art as a lens through which to teach multimodal literacy. Students were asked to compose analyses of graphic novels as well as try, to the best of their abilities, to create their own short graphic narratives. The class was a pilot course in my ongoing efforts to explore the use of comics and graphic novels in teaching multimodal literacy within the field of composition.[1] Multimodal literacy has become increasingly emphasized in composition and throughout English studies, as evidenced by the revised version of the "WPA Outcomes Statement for First-Year Writing" and the National Council of Teachers of English's (NCTE) "Position Statement on Multimodal Literacies." However, within this discourse, media such as websites, videos, blogs, newsletters, and podcasts are given much more attention than comics, which I argue are every bit as multimodal—and consequently just as important to teach. While I was using comics as the course's lens, my intention was to help the students draw larger connections about multimodal communication in general. So, while thinking critically about text-image relationships, students could extrapolate what they were learning and apply it in other contexts, such as analyses of advertisements, graphic design, or film. To be

A. Bourelle (✉)
University of New Mexico, Albuquerque, NM, USA

© The Author(s) 2018
A. Burger (ed.), *Teaching Graphic Novels in the English Classroom*,
DOI 10.1007/978-3-319-63459-3_2

honest, I was worried that students wouldn't fully grasp the connections I was asking them to make. I was pleasantly surprised when, in the end, they did. However, I was even more surprised by something else I learned teaching the course: the pedagogical value of focusing on graphic *narratives*, not necessarily graphic novels.

This experience made me realize that while comic books and graphic novels are becoming increasingly popular as culturally respected forms of entertainment and as literary works worthy of scholarly study, very little attention is being given to shorter graphic narratives. When people discuss comics, they typically think of ongoing series produced by comic book companies, or of stand-alone graphic novels. However, shorter graphic narratives are also widely and increasingly published. Graphic narratives— which I define as stand-alone comic stories somewhere in the range of one to twenty (or so) pages—are published in literary journals, as web comics, as stand-alone comic books, or even in newspapers. While the study and teaching of longer works (whether graphic fiction such as Alan Moore and Dave Gibbons' *Watchmen* or nonfiction such as Alison Bechdel's *Fun Home*) is certainly important, I argue that the shorter graphic narrative should not be ignored as a literary form worth studying and teaching. In this chapter, I explore the graphic narrative as a genre distinct from the graphic novel. In the same way fiction can be told in short story or novel form, or memoir can appear as an essay or full-length book, sequential art can be found in both long and short forms—graphic novels *and* graphic narratives.

My argument is framed by the experiences of students from the advanced composition course I taught, which was focused on the theme of comic books and multimodal literacy. Because students composed graphic narratives (not full-length graphic novels), most of the readings were graphic narratives. They learned to appreciate and understand the comic book/ sequential art/graphic novel genre broadly, as well as develop a greater understanding of multimodal literacy. They learned about the short form as well, coming to understand graphic narratives as a discrete literary art form, much like studying the short story is distinct from studying the novel. Moreover, by studying multiple examples of graphic narratives, students gained a broad understanding of the variety and range of storytelling and illustration techniques—much more so than if they were only looking at a few full-length graphic novels.

Through an analysis of students' reactions to course content, I argue that graphic narratives should not be overlooked in classes that emphasize graphic novels. While my observations come from an advanced composition course, with a focus on multimodal literacy, my argument is applicable to a much broader range of literature and English classes. My argument is not to teach the same class I did, in the same way (although that would be fine, too). Rather, my aim is for English instructors incorporating graphic novels into their courses, or instructors teaching courses devoted solely to comics/graphic novels, or instructors using graphic novels in some other pedagogical way, to be prompted and inspired to consider ways of emphasizing graphic narratives as well. When students learn about fiction, they don't only read novels. In fact, they would be ill-served if they did. They gain a broader, deeper, more critical understanding of the genre by looking at the spectrum possible within it, which includes the short story. In the same way, I argue, students benefit by seeing the spectrum possible with the genre of sequential art, which necessarily includes the graphic narrative.

WHY DIFFERENTIATE GRAPHIC NARRATIVES AND NOVELS?

As Jeet Heer and Kent Worcester point out in their *A Comics Studies Reader*, the term "comics" is filled with ambiguity, and therefore a variety of labels, including "graphic novels" and "graphic narratives," have been devised (xiii). Heer and Worcester point out that there are "divergent stances on how to talk about comics and whether the term is useful or valid" (xiii). I find it helpful to expose students to these divergent stances, asking them to wrestle with definitions. I think the discussions are ultimately more valuable than the definitions because the terms are often ambiguous and not agreed upon and the ability to critically analyze the genre should not be limited by this ambiguity.

To begin these discussions in the class I taught, I asked students to read excerpts from Scott McCloud's *Understanding Comics* and *Making Comics*, wherein McCloud provides terminology for students to discuss comics. One of the earliest readings was the part in *Understanding Comics* where McCloud defines what comics are: "Juxtaposed pictorial and other images in deliberate sequence intended to convey information and/or produce an aesthetic response in the viewer" (20). This definition, by McCloud's own explanation, excludes single-panel "cartoons," such as *Family Circus* (20–21), but includes instructional diagrams (20). As McCloud intends, the definition is debatable and functions as a start to the discussion of what comics are, not as the final word on the subject. I used the definition as a way to engage my students in a conversation about how they define comics. Like

Charles Hatfield in his article "Defining Comics in the Classroom; or, The Pros and Cons of Unfixability," I believe the goal of such discussions "is not to confirm one definition of comics above all others but to introduce students to questions of form and to show how different definitions serve different ends" (24). In other words, students benefit by discussing what they think comics are and considering the ways definitions of the genre can limit or misrepresent what they might think of as comics. I encourage students to reach their own definition of what comics are, a working definition that remains malleable and individual throughout the semester.

Discussions about the definition(s) of comics lead to more discussions about similar/synonymous definitions: sequential art, graphic novel, graphic memoir, comic book, comic series, comic strip, and so on. I approach these terms because, simply, students have likely heard some or all of them before and, if not, they will likely be exposed to them within the semester. Moreover, students might have predetermined biases about them. I've had one student who explained that he hated when graphic novels were called comic books, while another said he didn't understand why the term graphic novel was even necessary. He argued that "graphic novel" is just a new way of saying "comic books" because comics have historically been seen as inferior forms of literature. To use "graphic novel" as a replacement term because it sounds more respectable is to legitimize critics who think comic books are lesser works of art, he claimed.

I encourage my students not to get too hung up on these definitions. I follow Joseph Witek's advice in "Seven Ways I Don't Teach Comics" to not get bogged down by definitions (219–220). As Witek states, "Comics scholarship is a growing field, and its critical vocabulary is in constant flux" (219). However, I think it's important to discuss terms and definitions so that students can wrestle with the ideas of the genre they're studying. Part of the reason for discussing definitions is so students can see the limitations of various definitions.

One term I expose students to that they might not have heard before is "graphic narrative." While I don't mind if students don't adopt the term, I find it important to introduce it to them and try to use it to define a form of comics: specifically, short, stand-alone comics.[2] I do this for a few reasons. First, unlike "graphic novel" or "comic book," this is a term they likely haven't heard, and I think it's important to reveal it to them because it can be used to encompass a subgenre of which they might otherwise not be aware. Second, I believe the graphic narrative is discrete from the graphic novel, in the same way a short story is distinct from a novel. And third, and most importantly, I believe using graphic narratives to teach the genre of comics can be an invaluable way to show students the depth and breadth of possibilities available within the genre, including varying artistic styles and storytelling techniques.

In this essay, I am not necessarily advocating that readers, artists, and scholars adopt the term "graphic narrative." The term used to describe the short, stand-alone comic genre is of little importance to me compared to the value of teaching the short comics form to students. In the remainder of this essay, I will advocate for the inclusion of graphic narratives in curricula that attempt to teach comics/graphic novels, and I will discuss my own students' experiences when I did so.

What Do Students Learn from Graphic Narratives?

As I mentioned before, I asked my students to read from McCloud's *Understanding Comics* and *Making Comics*, which gave them a basis for understanding the broader genre, as well as a terminology for analyzing and discussing comics. Students learn basic vocabulary and concepts like "panel," "gutter," and "establishing shot," as well as more difficult concepts, such as the basic choices comic creators have (choice of moment, frame, image, word, and flow); different types of panel-to-panel transitions (moment-to-moment, action-to-action, subject-to-subject, scene-to-scene, aspect-to-aspect, and non sequitur); types of word-picture combinations (word-specific, picture-specific, duo-specific, intersecting, interdependent, parallel, and montage); and steps in the path of comic creation (idea/purpose, form, idiom, structure, craft, surface). While McCloud is quite effective at offering his own examples of these concepts, he provides them without context. So some of the concepts are difficult to fully understand from McCloud's examples alone. Just as one can't learn about fiction, poetry, or film simply by reading *about* them, students can't learn about comic books by only reading *about* them—they must read/view examples.

One benefit of using graphic narratives is that, because they are short, you can have students read a lot of them, thereby exposing them to many different styles and approaches. When students read a graphic novel, or a few graphic novels, they are exposed to some of these concepts at length, but not necessarily all of them. Allowing students to read a wide variety of short graphic narratives can provide just as much depth but even more breadth.

For example, when teaching students about the choice of flow, I showed them the example "Afterlife" by J. Bone, a four-page, full-color, wordless narrative that begins with the birth of the first living creatures on the planet and continues throughout the history of humankind. Instead of the traditional top-to-bottom, left-to-right flow of a typical comic, "Afterlife" follows a curving S-shaped flow, similar, in some ways, to the path of a board game. Students can follow the story easily and see that the typical panel structure is not the only way for a comic to flow from panel to panel. When teaching the concept of flow, I also used "Against the Flow" by Nick Sousanis. Published on a single full page of the *Boston Globe*, the comic explores "the connection between entropy and life" and, just like its title suggests, breaks away from the typical left-to-right, top-to-bottom flow of comics. Most of the comic is told through spiraling panels and images, prompting readers to read text circling toward the center of the page, and then circling back out. Sousanis's comic also shows unusual panel-to-panel transitions. As McCloud points out, most comic creators (at least those based in the United States) stick to a pretty regular pattern of panel transitions (*Understanding Comics* 75–76). Most comics use, in order of popularity, action-to-action, subject-to-subject, or scene-to-scene transitions. Therefore, other types of transitions—moment-to-moment, action-to-action, and non sequitur—are rarely found. In only one page (albeit a full newspaper page), Sousanis successfully uses all of the panel transitions.

These are just a few examples of the ways in which short graphic narratives can give students a broad understanding of various styles and techniques used in comics. Beyond showing the range of storytelling and composing styles, exposing students to such a wide variety also helps them see the range of subject matter that comics can address. Cecile de Rocher, in her essay "Working on Understanding Comics: Introducing the Teacher to the Graphic Narrative," states that graphic novels can be intimidating to prospective readers (22). Not only is the multimodal reading very different from reading a traditional text, but the subject matter might not be within someone's usual realm of taste. She states, "Part of people's nervousness comes from content that doesn't appeal" (22). "Some factions adore science- and speculative fiction," she continues, "while others thrive on the zombie theme or the surreal depictions of small-town life. The variety keeps growing and will surely continue to grow" (22–23). This variety is showcased in sharing short graphic narratives with students. While a student might not enjoy reading a several hundred-page graphic novel that is outside of her comfort zone, she will likely tolerate a few-page-long graphic narrative that takes her outside of her wheelhouse. And whether she appreciates it or not, she will quickly be able to move on to the next graphic narrative that might have a better chance of being interesting to her. In other words, because of their length, graphic narratives can be consumed in larger volumes than full-length graphic novels, increasing the chance that something students read will resonate.

In my class, I searched for the largest variety I could find. I included a full-color expository web comic explaining the role of climate change on the conflict in Syria (Quinn and Roche). I used short, abstract, poetic comics from Dave McKean's *Pictures that Tick*, which showcase a variety of black-and-white and fully painted artwork. I included comic versions of famous poems from the *Graphic Canon* books, such as William Shakespeare's "Sonnet 18" and Wilfred Owen's "Dulce et Decorum Est." I included coming-of-age stories by Michael Cho ("Stars," "Night Time"). I even included a graphic narrative by Isabella Rotman that tells the story of twenty million sperm, who have names and speak with dialogue bubbles, as they swim to fertilize an egg. (For a list of graphic narratives I've used—which is by no means an exhaustive list of graphic narratives available—please see the Appendix.) My goal was not only to expose students to art and storytelling techniques, but also to show them the depth of content possible within the comics genre. While asking students to read one, two, or even a few full-length graphic novels might accomplish this to some extent, exposing students to numerous, very different graphic narratives allowed me to show the extraordinary range of possibilities available within the genre.

How Do Graphic Narratives Contribute to Multimodal Literacy?

When instructors in composition or other English subfields adopt a pedagogy that includes multimodality, they ask students to learn to analyze media beyond traditional text-based papers. Pamela Takayoshi and Cynthia Selfe define multimodal texts as "texts that exceed the alphabetic and may include still and moving images, animations, color, words, music, and sound" (1). Graphic novels, which "combine print-text literacies with still image literacies" (Monnin 106), fall within this definition. Dale Jacobs states that, in comics, "meaning is created through print, visuals, and the combination of the two in order to achieve effects and meanings that would not be possible in either a strictly print or strictly visual text" (182). Jacobs explains that when he was a child "comics were a major site of literate practice, where [he] learned and practiced not only print literacy but also, and perhaps more importantly, multimodal literacy" (181).

Even though proponents of multimodal pedagogies often intend to promote digital literacies (see Brandt; Daley; Selfe), there are advocates who point out that multimodal literacy does not necessarily mean digital literacy (see Palmeri; Shipka). As Jody Shipka states, if instructors emphasize only the digital side of multimodal composition, "we risk missing or undervaluing the meaning-making and learning potentials" of other forms of multimodality (11). Jason Palmeri adds, "Although it is important to encourage students to recognize the power of alphabetic forms of communication, we also must help them come to understand that the written word (like all modalities) is limited in what it can discover and convey about the world" (158–9, his parentheses).

In a typical composition course, I would advocate the inclusion of some sort of comic or graphic narrative as a multimodal option. Graphic narratives are one of many multimodal genres students can study—and choose from— in a course addressing multimodality broadly. In such a course, perhaps a single graphic novel, or a few graphic narratives, would suffice as examples (just as one or two podcasts might represent that genre). However, in a class with a heavy emphasis on comics, such as the advanced composition course I taught, I argue that graphic narratives—not just graphic novels—should have an important role.

By exposing students to a wide variety and range of graphic narratives, students will gain a broader understanding of the possibilities of the genre, which, in turn, will provide a richer, deeper understanding of multimodal literacy. One of my students, in her end-of-semester reflection, stated that even though the course was focused on graphic narratives, she could see how what she learned was applicable to her life beyond the classroom.[3] She stated,

> [M]y major is in graphic design, which specializes in multimodal literacy. Graphic design covers anything from invitations and flyers to billboards and websites. It almost always consists of the use of both images and text laid out in a visually pleasing format. The assignments and information we covered in class will help me to understand the importance of the relationship between text and image. My rhetorical and multimodal literacy skills can be used for any medium and genre within my aspiring field.

She added that her "career after school has almost everything to do with the use of multimodal literacy and the lessons [she] learned during the course of this semester." She stated, "The skills I have gained in this class will help me both in finishing school and my career after college. I learned the importance of multimodal literacy in a number of mediums, and how the use of images alongside text can be very influential for your audience." For this particular student, who knew very little about comics before the semester began, the variety of graphic narratives, and the different approaches used to create them, was helpful in developing her multimodal literacy. She stated, "[D]ue to misconceptions during my early years, I thought that only nerdy boys read comics. This class opened my eyes to the variety of comics that are present in the world today." This reflection was particularly heartening for me as a teacher because the student not only learned to see the value of comics, but was also able to draw larger connections to her professional and academic life. She developed comic book literacy *and* multimodal literacy as a result of the course, which reinforced to me that my pedagogical approach was sound and effective.

Another student, a music major with a private business as a piano teacher, commented that the multimodal lessons about comics would help her advertise her business. She stated that she would in the future carefully consider what colors would be appealing and grab her audience's attention, as well as choose a font that was easy to read, looked professional, and was not "boring or stiff." She added, "Throughout the semester we've talked a lot about the relationship between images and text, and I will be able to apply that to choosing pictures to enhance an advertisement without taking away from the context and information [given] through the text." This student's comments illustrate how comics in general can contribute to multimodal literacies that extend beyond simply an understanding of comics. In the next section, I provide more student comments to showcase their reactions to reading multiple graphic narratives. Therefore, if readers are considering using graphic narratives but don't necessarily have the same multimodal-focused goals I did in my class, these comments should help show the value of using graphic narratives to teach generally about comic books. In other words, regardless of a teacher's goals when using comics in the classroom, I argue that there are important benefits to using multiple graphic narratives: specifically, to illustrate the range of possibilities within the genre.

What Do Students Say About Reading Graphic Narratives?

The advanced composition course I taught was themed "Comics and Multimodal Literacy," with a description posted on the English Department's website. Several students who enrolled were aware of the theme, but the majority had no idea what the focus was. Whether students had prior exposure to comics or were unfamiliar with the genre, they generally agreed that reading such a wide variety of graphic narratives helped them understand the full scope of the genre. One student who had not read many comics before stated, "It was always so nice to see the various styles of artwork throughout all the comics we read together as a class or on Blackboard online. Being able to read several comics and compare them afterwards really opened my eyes to a lot of things I wouldn't have noticed before." Another student, who said his exposure to comics before the class was limited to *Calvin and Hobbes,* stated, "I liked reading different types of comics in class and talking about them, it widened my view of the genre and showed me how to be more creative and think in a different way." With these two examples, the students specifically address the value of reading numerous comics and being able to compare them. In the case of students not particularly familiar with comics, using a variety seems like an ideal way to widen their view of the genre.

Another student unfamiliar with the genre stated that, by taking the class, he realized "that every choice a comic maker makes is extremely crucial to the comic's quality and how the comic is perceived by the audience." He added, "I learned this the most through the numerous comics we were required to read throughout the course of this class. As time went on, I began to notice myself paying attention to every detail of the comics in class." In this case, the student explicitly states that his broad understanding and appreciation of comics came as a result of "the numerous comics we were required to read." He concluded his comments by saying, "I will never look at or read a comic the same way again." Another student echoed these comments and stated that he could better understand the choices writers and artists make when creating comics: "I learned that thicker lines and lower colors aren't used just because that's what the artist of the comic had at hand; it was because the artist was trying to manipulate the mood of the text with images and color." These comments suggest the students noticed a level of detail in the comics *because* of the variety of comics they read. In other words, because they were able to compare and contrast so many examples, they noticed details within the comics that they might have overlooked otherwise.

Such comments weren't limited to students who were unfamiliar with comics. Other students who were self-described comic fans found that the variety and breadth of exposure to comics—made possible by reading so many short graphic narratives—helped them gain a greater understanding and appreciation of the genre. One student stated, "I took this class because I love comics, but despite being a pretty hardcore DC fan, I must say I learned much more about the world of comics then [sic] I expected!" The student stated that she "loved reading different genres of comics and analyzing them to a deeper degree." She concluded, "Reading them and discussing them helped me look at a comic in a different way." This student's comments suggest that even fans of comics benefited from the variety. In this case, the student said she was a fan of one particular publishing company, so it was helpful for her to see a wider range and variety of comics than what she was used to.

Another comic fan pointed out that the variety of graphic narratives gave him a greater appreciation of short comics—an appreciation that now extends to other shorter types of literature. Before the class, he stated, he always read ongoing series, only appreciating comic stories that were at least fifty pages, if not significantly longer. He stated, "I tended to pass over shorter comics as well as short stories in favor of something I believed to be more substantial and engaging. Now [...] I've come to appreciate shorter pieces of literature." The student stated that he always gravitated toward "more emotionally involved stories," and he generally avoided smaller comics and stories because he thought he would not be emotionally invested. "Comics [from the class] were all far more interesting than I anticipated," he stated, adding, "The dramatic shadows, emotional facial expressions, and incredibly engaging art style in each comic was more than enough to rewrite my opinion about short pieces of literature." This student's comments are particularly interesting because, as a teacher, I never anticipated that the comic selection would prompt students to appreciate genres outside of comics. However, this student not only gained an appreciation of shorter comics, but this caused him to rethink his bias toward shorter works in other forms. This was a side benefit I never foresaw.

Finally, there were also students who were not particularly interested in comic books at the beginning of class but who said they were now interested in seeking out graphic stories on their own. While gaining converts to the genre was not an explicit goal of the course, I think there is an underlying hope within classes focused on any sort of literature to foster an appreciation of the genre. So, as the teacher, I was certainly pleased when students mentioned they were new comic book fans. One student stated, "I have really enjoyed studying about comics, multimodal literacy, and rhetoric, and I believe that the things I have learned in this class will have an influence over my life for many years." She added, "I have also grown more interested in comics as a form of entertainment, and am interested in finding comics to read that would appeal to my interests, and discovering more about the artists and authors who create them." This student said this newfound appreciation was a result of the variety of comics she was exposed to: "My favorite thing that I learned from this class was that comics do not all fall into one category or genre." She stated that, before this class, she had always thought about comics as either being a "short cartoon comedy in the Sunday newspaper" or as a "series that contained lots of action and violence between superheroes and villains." "But," she stated, "after just a few weeks of class I began to see how comics can be used in so many different ways, and can be designed with any art style." She clearly learned more about the genre than she had known and, with her new appreciation, plans to continue reading comics, seeking out examples in line with her tastes. So, after studying comics in my class, she plans, in a sense, to continue to study the genre on her own. As a teacher, I'm not sure I would have accomplished this if I had only exposed students to a handful of full-length graphic novels.

These comments show that the students were surprised to find value in reading a variety of short graphic narratives. More than that, they were educated because of the variety. While these comments address students' general feelings about reading graphic narratives, I also want to provide a specific example of a graphic narrative I used. In the next section, I will focus on one particular graphic narrative that seemed to resonate with students.

What Is an Example of a Graphic Narrative and Its Impact on Students?

When it comes to word-picture relationships as described in McCloud's *Understanding Comics*, my students easily grasped the more obvious pairings, such as word-specific (where the text does most of the work) and picture-specific (where images do most of the work). However, when it came to some of the more complicated word-picture relationships, students needed examples to fully grasp the concepts. This was most apparent with montage, a word-picture relationship they really didn't understand from McCloud's explanation. With montage, the words are a part of the art itself. As an example, I showed students Isabella Rotman's "Sometimes I Have Feelings." The four-page black-and-white web comic became one of the students' favorite graphic narratives. The imagery shows a pair of hands wrestling with a dragon over a black background while white words twist around the images. The words tell the story, but they are not included in text bubbles over the images; rather, the words are actually a part of the artwork. The text describes the author/artist/narrator having feelings she hates and must tie up in a ball, dissect, and turn into a "very basic pain" she can then mold and sculpt into a story. The dragon in the pictures is a metaphor for the feelings she fights with and is able to turn into art.

After reading the narrative, students seemed to understand the concept of montage word-image relationships in a way they didn't before, but they also said the format—the way the words and images worked together seamlessly to create a distinct work of art—opened their eyes to the possibilities of graphic narratives. One student stated, "Before, I thought all comics were the same by having panels in a row along each page." The student added that Rotman's "Sometimes I Have Feelings" "had no panels and flowed through no set path. It was really refreshing to see a comic that had the text to be a part of the art and be completely different throughout the whole comic." This student's comments demonstrate that my goal of showing the montage word-picture relationship was accomplished, but more than that, the reading helped this student better understand the expansive possibilities within the genre of comic books. Another student, an avid comic book fan, stated that his favorite graphic narrative was "Sometimes I Have Feelings." "The visual aspect of this comic was just beautiful," he said, adding, "I loved the way the hands twisted and pulled the serpent that resembled her feelings." He added that he had never seen a comic in this format before, and after he read it in class, he went home and read it again. "It felt like I couldn't look away," he said. "It made sense to me and I loved the integration of words into the picture." Finally, another student added,

> While I did read a fair amount of comics prior to this course, they were all very strict in terms of what we might think of as traditionalism in comics. That is to say, they didn't stray far from the norm, and chose to keep text and dialogue in bubbles as well as minor boxes incorporated in or below each panel. But seeing the way that [Isabella Rotman] created organically flowing panels in *Sometimes I have Feelings* really spoke to me.

These comments demonstrate that even the students who knew a lot about comics could learn from the readings, and expand their appreciation of the genre. While not all the graphic narratives used in the class "really spoke to" every student, numerous students mentioned various comics and how they were educational or influential. This is one of the benefits of using graphic narratives: because they are short and you can ask students to read so many, most students will find one—or more—they connect with. So while I chose my graphic narratives because of what they could teach (I thought "Sometimes I Have Feelings" would be a good example of the montage word-picture relationship, for example), I was pleasantly surprised with the added benefit that it resonated so well with students.

I liken this to my own experience as an undergraduate student taking a class focused on reading short stories. I was an avid reader, but seeing the variety of possibilities within the genre of fiction opened my eyes in a new way. Like this student, some of the examples truly "spoke to me," which wasn't always the case when I took classes focused on reading a handful of longer works. I think the effect was similar here. Providing so many varied examples increased the chances that students would read something that resonated powerfully with them.

Conclusion: Will You Use Graphic Narratives in Your Classroom?

In this essay, I have argued that graphic narratives should not be ignored by those teaching comics and graphic novels. Just as teaching fiction should not focus exclusively on novels at the expense of short stories, teaching comics should not be limited to graphic novels at the expense of shorter graphic narratives. Teaching graphic narratives can help students develop their understanding of multimodal literacy, and it can give students a broader understanding—and appreciation—of the genre of comics. While I have described my discovery of the value of graphic narratives in the context of my specific advanced composition course focusing on multimodal literacy, I hope my advice is applicable to many other English, literature, or cross-disciplinary classes. I encourage teacher-scholars to take up my call to action to include more graphic narratives in comics/graphic novel studies. And I encourage instructors to think of new ways to invigorate their pedagogies with graphic narratives.

In *Making Comics*, McCloud states that creating comics requires making "a constant stream of *choices* regarding imagery, pacing, dialogue, composition, gesture, and a ton of other options" (9, original text in all caps, italics used for bold word). I argue that there is no better way to get students to see these choices than to expose them to a wide variety of graphic narratives. As one student stated, "Every single detail in a comic is chosen for a purpose, and I was unaware of that until I took this class." If the student had read only a small selection of lengthier graphic novels, perhaps that lesson might have gone unlearned.

Appendix

An incomplete list of graphic narratives that can be used for teaching the genre (complete bibliographic references in the Works Cited page):

"Hawaii 1997" by Sam Alden
"Lost and Found" by Lynda Berry
"I Love You" by Pascal Blanchet
"Afterlife" by J. Bone
"The Last Bullet" and "Winter Crossing" by Andrew Bourelle and Ed Bourelle
"Night Time" and "Stars" by Michael Cho
"The Grass Seed" by Claudia Dávila
"The Speaker" by Brandon Graham
"Dimensions" by Ted May
"Black Water," "Mixed Metaphors," and "His Story" by Dave McKean
"Red Eye" by Christoph Nieman
"Dulce et Decorum Est" by Wilfred Owen, adapted by Jason Cobley
"The Last Dragon," "Sometimes I Have Feelings," and "20,000,000" by Isabella Rotman
"Sonnet 18" by William Shakespeare, adapted by Robert Berry and Josh Levitas
"Against the Flow" by Nick Sousanis
"Bigger Blacker Kiss" by Sim

NOTES

1. See also my chapter "Multimodality 101: Graphic Narratives and Multimodal Composition" in the anthology *Class, Please Open Your Comics: Essays on Teaching with Graphic Narratives*, wherein I argue that comic books are multimodal and therefore can and should be taught in composition classes alongside other common multimodal projects such as websites, videos, podcasts, and brochures.

2. Barbara Postema, in *Narrative Structure in Comics: Making Sense of Fragments*, argues against the use of the term "graphic narrative" (as well as "graphic novel"), stating, "[T]here is a danger inherent precisely in creating a separation and disassociation between different kinds of comics genres, especially when the labels are ill-defined or haphazardly applied" (xi). However, I don't advocate using "graphic narrative" as an umbrella term for all comics, as Postema fears. Rather, I use it as a way to identify short graphic stories, whether fiction or nonfiction, as opposed to ongoing series or novel-length stand-alone books.

3. All student comments were obtained with IRB approval.

WORKS CITED

Alden, Sam. "Hawaii, 1997." *The Best American Comics 2014*, edited by Scott McCloud, Houghton Mifflin Harcourt, 2014, pp. 345–461.

Bechdel, Alison. *Fun Home: A Family Tragicomic*. Mariner Books, 2006.

Berry, Lynda. "Lost and Found." *How to Write Anything: A Guide and Reference with Readings*, edited by John J. Ruszkiewicz and Jay T. Dolmage, Macmillan, 2012, pp. 654–660.

Blanchet, Pascal. "I Love You." *Taddle Creek*, Christmas 2011, http://www.taddlecreekmag.com/i-love-you

Bone, J. "Afterlife." *Taddle Creek*, Summer 2009, http://www.taddlecreekmag.com/afterlife

Bourelle, Andrew. "Multimodality 101: Graphic Narratives and Multimodal Composition." *Class, Please Open Your Comics: Essays on Teaching with Graphic Narratives*, edited by Matthew L. Miller, McFarland Press, 2015, pp. 91–102.

Bourelle, Andrew, and Edward Bourelle. "The Last Bullet." *Heavy Feather Review*, vol. 3, no. 3 2014, pp. 47–50.

———. "Winter Crossing." *Stoneboat*, vol. 16, no. 1, 2015, pp. 50–57.

Brandt, Deborah. "Accumulating Literacy: Writing and Learning to Write in the Twentieth Century." *College English*, vol. 57, 1995, pp. 649–668.

Cho, Michael. "Night Time." *Taddle Creek*, Christmas 2004, http://www.taddlecreekmag.com/night-time

———. "Stars." *Taddle Creek*, Christmas 2007, http://www.taddlecreekmag.com/stars

Council of Writing Program Administrators. "WPA Outcomes Statement for First-Year Composition." *Wpacouncil.org*, 17 July 2014, http://wpacouncil.org/positions/outcomes.html

Daley, Elizabeth. "Expanding the Concept of Literacy." *Educause* March/April 2003, pp. 32–40.

Dávila, Claudia. "The Grass Seed." *Taddle Creek*, Summer 2008, http://www.taddlecreekmag.com/the-grass-seed

de Rocher, Cecile. "Working on Understanding Comics: Introducing the Teacher to the Graphic Novel." *Class, Please Open Your Comics: Essays on Teaching with Graphic Narratives*, edited by Matthew L. Miller, McFarland Press, 2015, pp. 21–29.

Graham, Brandon. "The Speaker." *The Best American Comics 2013*, edited by Jeff Smith, Houghton Mifflin Harcourt, 2013, pp. 26–34.

Hatfield, Charles. "Defining Comics in the Classroom; or, The Pros and Cons of Unfixability." *Teaching the Graphic Novel*, edited by Stephen E. Tabachnick, Modern Language Association, 2009, pp. 19–29.

Heer, Jeet, and Kent Worcester. *A Comics Studies Reader*. University Press of Mississippi, 2009. Jacobs, Dale. "Marveling at *The Man Called Nova*: Comics as Sponsors of Multimodal Literacy." *College Composition and Communication*, vol. 59, no. 2, 2007, pp. 180–205.

May, Ted. "Dimensions." *The Best American Comics 2014*, edited by Scott McCloud, Houghton Mifflin Harcourt, 2014, pp. 212–220.

McCloud, Scott. *Making Comics: Storytelling Secrets of Comics, Manga, and Graphic Novels*. New York, 2006.

———. *Understanding Comics: The Invisible Art*. William Morrow, 1993.

McKean, Dave. *Pictures that Tick*. Dark Horse Books, 2009.

Monnin, Katie. *Teaching Graphic Novels: Practical Strategies for the Secondary ELA Classroom*. Maupin House Publishing, 2010.

Moore, Alan, and Dave Gibbons. *Watchmen*. DC Comics, 1987.

National Council of Teachers of English. "Position Statement on Multimodal Literacies." *Ncte.org*, 2005, http://www.ncte.org/positions/statements/multimodalliteracies

Nieman, Christoph. "Red Eye." *The Best American Comics 2012*, edited by Françoise Mouly, Houghton Mifflin Harcourt, 2012, pp. 242–256.

Owen, Wilfred. "Dulce et Decorum Est." Jason Cobley (adapted by). *The Graphic Canon Vol. 3: From Heart of Darkness to Hemingway to Infinite Jest*, edited by Russ Kick, Seven Stories Press, 2013, pp. 173–180.

Palmeri, Jason. *Remixing Composition: A History of Multimodal Writing Pedagogy*. Southern Illinois University Press, 2012.

Postema, Barbara. *Narrative Structure in Comics: Making Sense of Fragments*. Rochester Institute of Technology, 2013.

Quinn, Audrey, and Jackie Roche. "What Is the Role of Climate Change in the Conflict in Syria?" *Upworthy*, 3 Sept. 2015, http://www.upworthy.com/what-is-the-role-of-climate-change-in-the-conflict-in-syria

Rotman, Isabella. "20,000,000." *Isabellarotman.com*, n.d.-a, http://www.isabella rotman.com/twentymillion

———. "The Last Dragon." *Isabellarotman.com*, n.d.-b, http://www.isabellaro tman.com/the-last-dragon

———. "Sometimes I Have Feelings." *Isabellarotman.com*, n.d.-c, http://www. isabellarotman.com/sometimesihavefeelings

Selfe, Cynthia L. "The Movement of Air, the Breath of Meaning: Aurality and Multimodal Composing." *College Composition and Communication*, vol. 60, no. 4, 2009, pp. 616–663.

Shakespeare, William. "Sonnet 18." Adapted by Robert Berry and Josh Levitas. *The Graphic Canon Vol. 1: From the Epic of Gilgamesh to Shakespeare to Dangerous Liaisons*, edited by Russ Kick. Seven Stories Press, 2013, pp. 406–416.

Shipka, Jody. *Toward a Composition Made Whole*. University of Pittsburgh Press, 2011.

Sim. "Bigger Blacker Kiss." *24 Hour Comics All-Stars*, edited by Nat Gertier, About Comics, 2005, pp. 212–238.

Sousanis, Nick. "Against the Flow." *Boston Globe*, 4 Oct. 2015, https://www.bo stonglobe.com/ideas/2015/10/03/sousanis/XOMd3JBYnEdzQCWHM6twTJ/ story.html

Takayoshi, Pamela and Cynthia L. Selfe. "Thinking About Multimodality." *Multimodal Composition: Resources for Teachers*, edited by Cynthia L. Selfe, Hampton Press, 2007, pp. 1–12.

Witek, Joseph. "Seven Ways I Don't Teach Comics." *Teaching the Graphic Novel*, edited by Stephen E. Tabachnick. Modern Language Association, 2009, pp. 217–222.

CHAPTER 3

Understanding Rhetoric, Understanding Genre: A Rhetorical Genre Studies Approached Writing Course

Sara Austin

A rhetorical genre studies approach is an ideal fit for an intermediary writing class designed to explore intersections of genre and rhetoric. Using the textbooks *Understanding Rhetoric* and *The Bedford Book of Genres*, my course asks students to consider the genres in which they write in their major, as well as genres they may encounter in future careers beyond the university. As a result of this approach, the course endeavors to move away from traditional forms of argumentation and persuasion through an examination of alternative rhetorical theories.

Designed as a bridge that could serve as an introduction to a writing minor, the rhetorical genre studies approach offers students the opportunity to practice and design future genres they will encounter. It might serve as an elective that can be added to a writing program or existing writing curriculum. The main goal for this course is to provide practical writing experiences for writing on the job or writing in the disciplines. The rhetorical genre studies approach is one that allows tailoring by each student for their writing needs and interests, and the textbook *Understanding Rhetoric: A Graphic Guide to Writing* by Elizabeth Losh, Jonathan Alexander, Kevin Cannon, and Zander Cannon offers students an alternative approach to a

S. Austin (✉)
Bowling Green State University, Bowling Green, OH, USA

© The Author(s) 2018
A. Burger (ed.), *Teaching Graphic Novels in the English Classroom*,
DOI 10.1007/978-3-319-63459-3_3

traditional textbook while simultaneously introducing one of the possible genres for future study. With this in mind, the learning outcomes of the course are to

1. Demonstrate awareness of rhetorical theories and their applications;
2. Master a variety of genres, both academic and non-academic;
3. Observe and analyze the role audience plays in genre creation and perception;
4. Evaluate differing characteristics and purposes between genres;
5. Identify and describe various features and patterns of genres;
6. Enlarge and adapt composing processes to various writing tasks and genres;
7. Analyze genres within fields, share this knowledge, and use it to broaden and develop writing habits; and
8. Produce finished project conforming to guidelines of a style manual.

The assignment and activity requirements of the course to accomplish the learning outcomes are to read and discuss thematically arranged texts from a critical perspective as sources for understanding rhetorical theory, genre, and writing; study and practice rhetorical theories in the development of writing tasks; complete writing tasks that require summary, analysis, synthesis, and/or interpretation of rhetorical theory and genres; apply rhetorical theory to writing tasks; and use style manual guidelines and genre conventions in the preparation of the final genre project.

In order to accomplish these goals and learning outcomes, this course takes a different approach than the traditional focus on argument and persuasion. Since argumentation and persuasion are often privileged genres in the composition classroom, though representing only a fraction of what rhetoric can do, they often receive the most treatment in textbooks. Even as textbooks elaborate on definitions of argumentation by including alternatives such as Rogerian argument and invitational rhetoric, argument and persuasion continue as the gold standard. Because persuasion and argumentation only represent a small portion of many genres students encounter during their time in college and beyond, facilitating transfer to other genres becomes increasingly important. For these reasons, two textbooks are utilized in this course: *Understanding Rhetoric* and *The Bedford Book of Genres*. The use of these two texts is framed through a lens of invitational rhetoric as proposed by Sonja Foss and Cindy Griffin's "Beyond Persuasion: A Proposal for Invitational Rhetoric." In addition to these textbooks, the course is supplemented with additional readings on stasis, invention, invitational rhetoric, and genre theory. Teaching these rhetorical strategies as a means to encounter other genres and move beyond argument and persuasion provides a practical approach to transfer, as it encourages students to look beyond work in the class. Rather than defeating an opponent, stasis theory and invitational rhetoric allow other types of argumentation and genre to be valued in the composition classroom. *Understanding Rhetoric* provides a great starting point to build on for this approach. For example, "Issue 4: Argument Beyond Pro and Con" presents a more traditional approach to argument that can then be built off of and included in a discussion of invitational rhetoric; since much of this chapter focuses on creating effective arguments in an academic writing context, it provides a reframing of information that many students are already familiar with from previous First Year Composition (FYC) courses.

The theoretical approach for this course is primarily structured around Foss and Griffin's 1995 article "Beyond Persuasion: A Proposal for Invitational Rhetoric," which calls for a more inclusive rhetorical approach in both theory and practice. Although met with much criticism from scholars, their outlined call for rhetorical approaches beyond persuasion mirrors and complements other theorists, such as Carl Rogers. Foss and Griffin's proposed invitational rhetoric, which expands upon a more traditional understanding of rhetoric, is defined as "an invitation to understanding as a means to create a relationship rooted in equality, immanent value, and self-determination ... [which] constitutes an invitation to the audience to enter the rhetor's world and see it as the rhetor does" (5). This approach bears many similarities to Rogerian rhetoric in allowing audience members to create understanding of viewpoints rather than listening to opposing views, in order to make an argument stronger. Although several scholars (M. Lane Bruner, Catherine Helen Palczewski, Richard Fulkerson, among others) have heavily criticized Foss and Griffin's invitational rhetoric for presenting a "bifurcation of rhetorical strategies into gendered categories that reify dichotomous gender interactions" or "as a rejection of argumentation as a viable or ethical rhetorical tool," Foss and Griffin's approach augments many feminist rhetorical approaches (Meyer 8). Taking these concerns by scholars into account, it is important to note my reasoning for framing this course through an invitational rhetoric lens.

To begin with, the majority of first-year composition courses deal with argumentation and persuasion as a staple of the curriculum. So, as an elective intermediate writing course, the rhetorical principles of this genre-based course are building on those that have been studied in a first-year course. This doesn't represent a dichotomous approach with the intention of reifying gender interactions, but rather an augmented representation that introduces various alternatives to persuasion and argumentation. By building on Foss and Griffin's call, which first outlines rhetoric as persuasion and then expands on feminist rhetorical theory in the proposal of invitational rhetoric, this course presents students with an invitation to see writing tasks from multiple perspectives. This move to extend rhetoric beyond persuasion seeks to avoid "the act of changing others [which] not only establishes the power of the rhetor over others but also devalues the lives and perspectives of those others" (Foss and Griffin 3). One of the primary goals of this course, then, is to place more value on the lives and perspectives of students and the types of writing students do in various academic and non-academic contexts. Foss and Griffin further their rhetorical approach by calling on principles of feminist rhetoric such as equality, immanent value, and self-determination. These three principles emphasize the need for an understanding necessary to create relationships of equality, grounded in the core belief that each student is unique and has value in their perspective. Including self-determination in this approach ensures the course is grounded in respect for others and acknowledges that students are authorities on their own lives, that each student makes decisions about their own writing and constitutes their worlds as they choose. The invitational rhetoric framing attempts to move beyond understanding of the issue to a non-hierarchical, non-judgmental, and non-adversarial approach that highlights mutual understanding of perspectives. For these reasons, invitational rhetoric offers a distinct approach and enhances a rhetorical genre studies approach to writing, as this course encourages writers to "simultaneously bring multiple knowledge domains—subject matter, rhetorical knowledge, discourse community knowledge, and writing process knowledge—into dynamic interaction" (Barawashi and Reiff 192).

The dynamic interaction present in this course is represented by the structure. The course is divided into two halves: the first is heavily centered on rhetorical concepts and theories presented in *Understanding Rhetoric*. Frontloading the readings from *Understanding Rhetoric* in the first half of the semester provides students with a refresher of information from first-year courses that can be built upon as a way to introduce alternative genres to academic writing and other types of writing beyond argument or persuasion. Specifically, focusing on the chapters that highlight genre in the textbook serves as an introduction to the importance of rhetorical genre studies and the genres that will be studied in the second half of the course.

Understanding Rhetoric offers several chapters that help emphasize the learning outcomes. "Issue 2: Strategic Reading" reinforces the importance of strategic reading through investigating texts, reading strategies, synthesis, and audience awareness. This emphasis on reading provides a precursor to the types of genre analysis that happen later in the semester. Similarly, "Issue 3: Writing Identities" gives students the opportunity to consider their identities as writers before proposing a genre project that will be most useful to a scholarly or workplace identity. Since this course is an elective, the chapter on research, "Issue 5: Research: More than Detective Work," allows for a shift in the conversation about types of research. As everything in the course works toward the final genre project, the opportunity to revisit types of sources beyond the persuasive or argumentative research projects students would have produced in other writing courses is necessary to consider. Additionally, this variation allows students to consider how sources are used in different genres and, from there, the conversation can shift to the types of sources needed for the type of genre project the student wishes to create. "Issue 6: Rethinking Revision" also fits in nicely with an invitational rhetoric framing, as it invites students to read rhetorically and see through others' eyes. This is especially important for this course, as students will be creating different genre projects from one another, so understanding the type of work classmates are doing becomes increasingly important for peer review sessions and workshops.

The graphic format of *Understanding Rhetoric* works especially well for this course as it echoes the shift in emphasis away from argumentation and persuasion. Just as the course takes a non-traditional approach in the content, *Understanding Rhetoric* provides students with an alternative approach to a writing textbook. The visual emphasis of the textbook highlights genres of writing, publishing, and scholarship that differ from traditional textbook alternatives in a format with which students are already familiar. From a pedagogical perspective, "The graphic approach of *Understanding Rhetoric* supports instructors who want to teach with a book that ... is both visually and textually rich" (Losh et al. vi). The inclusion of the "Reframe" section at the end of each issue provides students with tangible connections to their writing lives, opportunities for class discussion, and assignments that engage students in examples outside the classroom. The visual and textual richness of *Understanding Rhetoric* is echoed not only in the assignments and final genre project, but also through a pedagogical framing that invites students to grapple and work with genres with which they may not be familiar.

The graphic novel approach also gives students the opportunity to familiarize themselves with rhetorical concepts in a familiar, approachable way before additional rhetorical theories are introduced later in the course. The theoretical framing of the course informs both its objectives and its content. In addition to *Understanding Rhetoric*, the course is supplemented with additional readings. During the first half of the semester, students spend time on rhetorical theories and concepts. For each of the major rhetorical theories covered in the first half of the course (genre, invention, stasis, and invitational rhetoric), the students write a rhetorical brief. The purpose of these briefs is to synthesize each theory and demonstrate understanding and application, highlighting how the theories connect together to form a broader understanding of rhetorical theories and their applications. These briefs may also eventually be used to rationalize the end of semester genre project.

The first rhetorical brief covers genre, but more specifically introduces rhetorical genre studies in order to emphasize the connection between genre and rhetoric. The definition of genre employed comes from *The Bedford Book of Genres*, which provides a concise overview, as well as the opening "A Theory of Genre" chapter of Amy Devitt's *Writing Genres*, and "Rhetorical Genre Studies" from *Genre: An Introduction to History, Theory, Research, and Pedagogy*. Following genre, the next rhetorical theory covered is invention. Discussion of invention early in the semester highlights the importance of practicing rhetorical theories in the development of writing tasks, as well as the application of rhetorical theory to writing tasks themselves so that the composing process can be enlarged and adapted. Including invention encourages students to move beyond the traditional prewriting and brainstorming modeling of invention and provides practical techniques to use, as strategies are considered for selecting the genre for their final genre project. Although some of the readings on invention are selected from the Purdue OWL site and do include traditional prewriting techniques, there are additional readings, including "Reinventing Invention," a selection from *Writing Spaces: Readings on Writing*. Invention is then followed by stasis theory, which gives students more opportunity to understand different types of genres, the roles they play, and how to build bridges rather than dig trenches (Brizee). This discussion of stasis theory is fueled by a need to "assist rhetors in identifying the central issues in given controversies, and in finding the appropriate argumentative topics useful in addressing these issues" (Sloan). The goal in including stasis theory is to provide students with tools to identify misunderstandings that may arise between genres and ways to move beyond them.

Appropriately, following stasis comes a discussion of alternatives to argument, including invitational rhetoric and Rogerian rhetoric. Of these two theories, students have the option to choose one on which to focus their final rhetorical brief. Because invitational rhetoric provides the framing for the course as a whole, it is important to implement some of Foss and Griffin's proposed alternatives by giving students equitable options. As discussed earlier, invitational rhetoric moves to examine forms of rhetoric other than persuasion or argument and, in a course focused on genre, an examination of other definitions should be included to present alternatives to expansive definitions of argument that are often presented "as another form of traditional argument, one that privileges argument as winning and undercuts the radical potential of argument as understanding across differences" (Knoblauch 245). I. A. Richards' definition of old rhetoric also fits into this framing: "Perhaps what it has most to teach us is the narrowing and binding influence of that preoccupation, that debaters' interest. Persuasion is only one among the aims of discourse" (Richards 1281). With the inclusion of Rogerian rhetoric and invitational rhetoric, students have the opportunity to seek understanding and examine other aims of discourse. The inclusion of more than one alternative to argument and persuasion is a central component of the course and an appropriate final rhetorical brief assignment, as it serves as an introduction to other aims of discourse that are present in various genres.

Because the course and the readings are drawing on Foss and Griffin's theory of invitational rhetoric, including a variety of readings from multiple sources makes the readings more customizable depending on the student population of the course. Many of the supplemental readings could be substituted for readings from *Writing about Writing* or similar writing textbooks that offer a rhetorical framework.

The second half of the semester moves from a focus on rhetorical theory to more in-depth exploration of various genres across disciplines using the textbook *The Bedford Book of Genres*. The goal of the second half of the semester is to emphasize the rhetorical nature of different genres and allow students to explore the rhetoric of various genres within their majors or future careers. The genres examined in the second half of the course include a variety of academic and non-academic sources. A way to emphasize the rhetorical nature of genres that students are already familiar with is by having students bring in similar pieces from their first-year writing courses to examine genre conventions, audience expectations, and similarities and differences across a similar genre. From there, more non-academic sources are included, such as blogs, emails, cover letters and resumes, reports, and collaborative genres, among others.

Following "Guidelines for Analyzing Genres" from Anis S. Bawarshi and Mary Jo Reiff's *Genre: An Introduction to History, Theory, Research, and Pedagogy*, the connection of rhetoric and genre should be clear, as patterns of genre, rhetorical features, and purposes are studied and examined for each genre (Bawarshi and Reiff 193). This provides a practical examination of genres through the lens of rhetorical genre studies. The readings in the second half of the semester are also supplemented with examples of genres that serve to fill out the genre studies approach and give students a variety of genres to study and with which to familiarize themselves.

The rhetorical genre studies approach culminates in the final genre project, in which students propose and create within a genre that will be academically or professionally useful to them. This project requires students to become experts in their chosen genre, collect samples, explain how the genre is used, and then create a version of that genre that demonstrates their knowledge. The genre project consists of a proposal where students outline ideas for the project and how it relates to interests, studies, or types of writing the student wishes to explore. The proposal then develops into a rationale that outlines how the project came to be, including its purpose, uses, and relevance to the student. Additionally, each student presents on their genre of choice at the end of the semester and an abstract describing the project accompanies the presentation as a handout for other students. The genre project also encourages students to develop a critical awareness of genre while teaching students how to move beyond some genre conventions and produce alternatives (Bawarshi and Reiff 200). The genre project also provides students with the opportunity to combine genres and "discover that there's more than one way to respond to a situation" (Bawarshi and Reiff 201). This course would also be a good candidate for incorporating ethnographic approaches such as "participant/observation research of communities in order to enable students to examine and to see first-hand how communities use genres to carry out social actions and agendas" (Bawarshi and Reiff 203). Importantly, the genre project gives students the option for a multimodal project. Because of the other components present in the project (proposal, abstract, rationale, and presentation), creating a project that is multimodal allows for more opportunities for meaning making and transfer.

As the multimodal project creates opportunities for visual and artistic representations, one option that students might consider is a graphic novel or visual component in their project, further building on representations that students have familiarized themselves with through *Understanding Rhetoric*. The textbook especially lends itself to these types of assignments: "By emphasizing multimodal approaches to composing, we wanted to engage student writers in thinking about their identities, contexts for their research, and effective writing processes" (Losh et al. v).

Overall, this course builds on concepts students have encountered in other first-year writing courses, so there is minimal overlap, and introduces new material that is grounded in a rhetorical genre studies approach. In creating the final genre project, as much choice as possible is put in the hands of the students, encouraging them to critically reflect and consider the types of writing they do and ways in which the project can transfer to their core classes, future writing, and careers.

Appendix A: Genre Project

Assignment Overview

Your Genre Project will give you the opportunity to explore and apply what we have learned this semester about the intersection of rhetoric and genre and the rhetoric of your major. Moving into the second half of the semester, we will be examining genres across multiple disciplines, both within and beyond the academy. While we explore these genres, you will become more familiar with types of genres and cultivate a working knowledge of the genres you see yourself working with the most in the future. Therefore, this project will allow you to start with the genres we explore in class, of which you will choose one as a jumping off point for your final project. You may choose to create a project based on a genre we study in class, or you may decide to create a genre of your own. This could be a blend of genres, or a specific genre that forms into something more useful to you. Additionally, if your genre is natively digital or multimodal, your final project can be digital or multimodal.

In researching your genre, you will familiarize yourself with the genre's function, setting, subject, participants, and purpose. You should consider all of these factors in crafting your final project, as well as the formatting, design, and presentation of your genre. As you research your genre, pay attention to the rhetorical situation, and the rhetorical appeals being used. Additionally, look for opportunities where stasis theory and invitational rhetoric can be used in your genre project to facilitate understanding and build bridges across disciplines: how can these rhetorical theories allow you to fairly represent your genre project and understand the genre projects of your peers?

Your genre project will include five components:

Proposal: 500–750 words (2–3 pages or digital equivalent)
> Your proposal will give you an opportunity to discuss any ideas you have for the genre project as it relates to your interests, major, or types of writing that will be most useful to you. Because it comes relatively early (Week 12) in our overview of genres, you are not necessarily committed to the project you discuss in your proposal.

Abstract: Approximately 250 words (1 page)
> The abstract is a short description of your genre project. It will be due when you give your presentation so your classmates have an overview of your project.

Rationale: 750–1000 words (3–4 pages or digital equivalent)
> The rationale for your project will be a more developed version of your proposal in which you discuss how you chose your project, its uses, and its relevance to future writing, career, major, etc.

Project: 1500–2000 words (6–8 pages or digital equivalent)
> This is where you create a version of your genre and identify, describe, and analyze the patterns, rhetorical situation, how it is used, etc. Your total project, including your version of your genre, will be a total of 6–8 pages, so depending on the length, formatting, and design of your project, the description and analysis portion can vary in length. Please note that you are responsible for understanding formatting guidelines for your genre and its conventions.

Presentation: 15–20 minutes
> Your presentation will explain your chosen genre, what your project accomplishes, and how it fits within and moves beyond conventions.

Deadlines

Week 12: Genre Proposal Due
Week 13: Instructor Conferences
Week 14: Peer Review
Weeks 15–16: Presentations (Abstract Due with Your Presentation)
Week 16 (Day of Final): Genre Project Due (Rationale and Project)

Assessment

Project	30 points
Knowledge of genre	20 points
Genre analysis (including rhetorical connection)	20 points
Style, formatting, and design	10 points
Presentation, abstract, proposal, rationale	(5 points each) 20 points
Total points possible	100 points

APPENDIX B: SAMPLE SCHEDULE

Week	Agenda	Assignment due
1	Introduction to course, genre, types of writing you do **Introduction to rhetoric** *Understanding Rhetoric* Introduction and Issue 1	
2	**Understanding texts** *Understanding Rhetoric* Issue 2 **Introduction to genre** *Bedford Book of Genres* Chapter 1 Devitt—"A Theory of Genre"	
3	**Genre continued** "Rhetorical Genre Studies" **Invention** "Introduction and Overview"	**Genre rhetorical brief**
4	**Invention continued** "Introduction to Prewriting," "Reinventing Invention" **Writing identities** *Understanding Rhetoric* Issue 3	**Invention rhetorical brief**
5	**Stasis theory** "Stasis Introduction" and "Stasis and Research" **Moving beyond argument** *Understanding Rhetoric* Issue 4	**Stasis rhetorical brief**
6	**Invitational rhetoric** Foss and Griffin—"Beyond Persuasion: A Proposal for Invitational Rhetoric" **Rogerian rhetoric** Rogers—"Communication", Teich—"Rogerian Problem-solving and the Rhetoric of Argumentation"	**Invitational/Rogerian rhetoric rhetorical brief**
7	**Making the genre work for you** "Navigating Genres" **The genre of your discipline** Course syllabus from a core class	

(*continued*)

Week	Agenda	Assignment due
8	**What should I know about my genre?** *Understanding Rhetoric* Issue 6 **Narrative genres** *Bedford Book of Genres* Chapter 2	
9	**Informative genres** *Bedford Book of Genres* Chapter 3 **Persuasive genres** *Bedford Book of Genres* Chapter 4	
10	**What should I know about my genre?** *Understanding Rhetoric* Issue 6 **Exploring topics & creating proposals** *Bedford Book of Genres* Chapter 5	
11	**Composing in genres** *Bedford Book of Genres* Chapter 8 **The genre of remixing** *Bedford Book of Genres* Chapter 8	
12	**Multigenre projects** *Bedford Book of Genres* Chapter 10 **The genre of revision** *Understanding Rhetoric* Issue 7	Genre proposal
13	**The genre of collaboration** *Understanding Rhetoric* Issue 5 **Exploring topics & creating proposals** *Bedford Book of Genres* Chapter 5	
14	**Moving forward with your genre** *Understanding Rhetoric* Issue 8 **Presentations**	Abstract due with your presentation
15	**Presentations** **Presentations**	Abstract due with your presentation Abstract due with your presentation
16		Genre project due

Works Cited

Bawarshi, Anis S. and Mary Jo Reiff. *Genre: An Introduction to History, Theory, Research, and Pedagogy.* Parlor Press, 2010.

Braziller, Amy and Elizabeth Kleinfeld. *The Bedford Book of Genres: A Guide & Reader.* Bedford/St. Martin's, 2014.

Brizee, H. Allen. "Stasis Theory as a Strategy for Workplace Teaming and Decision Making." *Journal of Technical Writing and Communication*, vol. 38, no. 4, 2008, pp. 363–85.

Bruner, M. Lane. "Producing Identities: Gender Problematization and Feminist Argumentation." *Argumentation and Advocacy*, vol. 32, no. 4, Spring 1996, pp. 185–98.

Devitt, Amy. "A Theory of Genre." *Writing Genres.* Southern Illinois UP, 2004, pp. 1–33.

Foss, Sonja and Cindy Griffin. "Beyond Persuasion: A Proposal for Invitational Rhetoric." *Communication Monographs*, vol. 62, 1995, pp. 2–18.

Fulkerson, Richard. "Transcending Our Conception of Argument in Light of Feminist Critiques." *Argument and Advocacy*, vol. 32, no. 4, Spring 1996, pp. 199–217.

Knoblauch, A. Abby. "A Textbook Argument: Definitions of Argument in Leading Composition Textbooks" *College Composition and Communication*, vol. 63, no. 2, 2011, pp. 244–68.

Losh, Elizabeth, Jonathan Alexander, Kevin Cannon, and Zander Cannon. *Understanding Rhetoric: A Graphic Guide to Writing.* 2nd ed., Bedford/St. Martin's, 2017.

Meyer, Michaela D. E. "Women Speak(ing): Forty Years of Feminist Contributions to Rhetoric and an Agenda for Feminist Rhetorical Studies." *Communication Quarterly*, vol. 55, no. 1, 2007, pp. 1–17.

Palczewski, Catherine Helen. "Argumentation and Feminism: An Introduction." *Argumentation and Advocacy*, vol. 32, no. 4, Spring 1996, pp. 161–69.

Richards, I. A. "From *The Philosophy of Rhetoric*." *The Rhetorical Tradition: Readings from Classical Times to the Present.* 2nd ed., edited by Patricia Bizzell and Bruce Herzberg, Bedford/St. Martin's, 2001, pp. 1281–94.

Sloan, Thomas O. "Stasis." *Encyclopedia of Rhetoric,* Vol. 1. Oxford UP, 2001.

Trim, Michelle D. and Megan Lynn Isaac. "Reinventing Invention: Discovery and Investment in Writing." *Writing Spaces: Readings on Writing.* Vol. 1, edited by Charles Lowe and Pavel Zemilansky, Parlor Press, 2010, pp. 107–25.

CHAPTER 4

Writing Through Comics

Riki Thompson

Graphic textbooks such as *The Manga Guide to Physics*, *The Manga Guide to Calculus*, and *Understanding Rhetoric: A Graphic Guide to Writing* reflect a growing acceptance of non-traditional texts as teaching tools that can help students understand complex ideas. The recent publication of Nick Sousanis's *Unflattening* as an important piece of scholarship, originally a Columbia University doctoral dissertation written in the form of a graphic novel, shows an even greater level of acceptance of this form, demonstrating how the relationship between words, pictures, literature, and perception are important to how we construct knowledge.

Comics and graphic novels are often thought of as simpler versions of their text-only counterparts and, by extension, have not been given the respect or recognition they deserve. In Scott McCloud's *Understanding Comics*, he argues for the evaluation of comics as a significant form of literature and art, deserving of respect. In his sequel, *Reinventing Comics: How Imagination and Technology Are Revolutionizing an Art Form*, McCloud traces the lineage of comics and points to the birth of the graphic

I wanted to thank my students of Spring TWRT 333 who agreed to share their reflections on writing through comics for this collection. Thanks to Soyoung Choi, Sage Farray, Lucas Gomez, Jill Grove, Marcela Martine, Olga Subbotin, and Molly Ubben.

R. Thompson (✉)
University of Washington Tacoma, Tacoma, WA, USA

© The Author(s) 2018
A. Burger (ed.), *Teaching Graphic Novels in the English Classroom*,
DOI 10.1007/978-3-319-63459-3_4

43

novel as monumental in changing the status of the genre, stating that in "moving from periodical to *book*, an implicit claim of *permanent worth* was being made—a claim that had to be justified" (29, emphasis original), compared to the "temporary worth" associated with periodicals. McCloud makes a compelling case for how many modern comics are incorporating the features of great writing while masterfully employing strategies that are distinct to comics writing.

Comics studies is much like the field of film studies a few decades ago: questioned in terms of its rigor and appropriateness for the high-minded goals of the college classroom due to a focus on spectacle and mediated forms used for entertainment value. Like film, comics are an important literary form that represent everyday life, relying upon common tropes to tell stories of love, loss, connection, growth, personal development, and morality lessons about good and evil. In "Visual Literacy, to comics or not to comics?," Leone Tiemensa argues that comics are an important medium for improving literacy as they combine printed words and pictures to represent narrative in today's increasingly visual world. In "More than Words: Comics as a Means of Teaching Multiple Literacies," Dale Jacobs argues that comics are complex, multimodal texts that can engage students in multiple literacies. Both Heidi Kay Hammond and M. G. Aune argue that teaching comics conventions through graphic novel close reading improves multimodal literacy skills. Part of the task of teaching students to write with comics is to teach them the demanding task of close reading. In writing courses that integrate learning objectives aimed at visual rhetoric and close reading, using comics is a natural fit. While comics may be simply understood as "sequential art," the more complex definition of them as "juxtaposed pictorial and other images in deliberate sequence" (McCloud, *Understanding Comics* 150) points to their significance as a storytelling tool.

There has been a trend to integrate comics into college classrooms to meet a variety of teaching objectives. Land Dong's *Teaching Comics and Graphic Narratives: Essays on Theory, Strategy and Practice* provides numerous examples of how to use comics to teach for a variety of disciplines such as American Studies, Ethnic Studies, Gender Studies, Cultural Studies, and Communication, as well as Composition and Rhetoric Studies. The overriding practice for bringing comics into the classroom is to focus on close reading and critique. Even in composition and rhetoric courses, comics and graphic novels are used as reading content that informs analytical essays of some sort. And while teachers espouse the importance of integrating comics to teach multimodal literacy and prepare students for the jobs they will do after college, Katharine Polak Macdonald suggests that "most students during college and in their career will be producing multimodal texts far more often than traditional texts, since the workplace becomes increasingly digitized" (226).

Despite arguments that students need the skills to produce the types of texts that are becoming more common in the digital age, college courses remain conservative in how they approach this task. Many have found ways to teach reading skills, but few have ventured into teaching both reading and production. Overwhelmingly, assignments reflect attention to reading practices, not writing practices. It is likely that finding ways to integrate this into the curriculum is part of the obstacle, as is teachers' discomfort with their own ability to write through comics. McDonald argues, "multimodal texts, especially those we see on the Internet in the form of YouTube videos and blogs with multi-genre content, are now commonplace. This is important to understand as teachers who are preparing students for the production of their own texts in the 'real world,' particularly because our notions of literacy can sometimes valorize outdated models of texts" (222).

In this case study, I reflect on an upper-division course, Writing through Comics, developed for the interdisciplinary program at the University of Washington Tacoma, an urban-serving university in the Pacific Northwest. Our school recently created a Writing Studies major that prepares students "to be verbally and visually literate, encouraging [their] growth as a learner, citizen and professional" (University of Washington Tacoma, "Writing Studies"). This course targets the learning objectives focused on helping students learn to think critically and creatively and to write effectively for a variety of purposes in a wide range of genres. Writing through Comics was proposed as part of the larger and ongoing vision to diversify the genre-based course offerings in the Creative Writing track by making courses both more reflective of contemporary publishing trends and also more consistent with the interdisciplinary mission of our school. Because Comics Studies is a burgeoning interdisciplinary field that draws on the traditions of creative writing, visual design, art, rhetoric, and new media studies, this course offers a unique opportunity for students to explore the art and craft of comics writing while offering them a creative-writing experience that crosses disciplinary boundaries.

According to the "Mission, Values, and Vision Statement" for the University of Washington Tacoma's School of Interdisciplinary Arts and Science, the curricular goals of our school are interdisciplinary in nature, with our first goal focused on helping students "Develop proficiency in skills such as writing and critical thinking that are needed for productive careers, and gain mastery of a broad curriculum in the humanities, social sciences and environmental science" (University of Washington Tacoma, "SIAS Mission, Vision and Values | UW Tacoma"). In addition, we look to help students "gain a knowledge and appreciation of cultures other than their own while exploring the expression of cultural identity, thought and beliefs through literature and the other arts." With these goals in mind, this course aims to teach students to be critical thinkers who can close read texts, understand how these texts fit in the world, and compose meaningful pieces of writing using skills transferable to life beyond college. Thus, the student learning goals for the course are broadly aimed at teaching students critical thinking and writing skills simultaneously. From the interpretive side, activities and assignments teach students to become critical readers of these non-traditional literary texts, paying close attention to how visual and written elements contribute to storytelling. Once students learn to close read published comics, interpretive practices are applied to the writing process by workshopping specific aspects of design and storytelling through the process of drafting, reviewing, and revising a comic.

Interpretive Skills

The greatest challenge of this course is balancing the need to teach analytical interpretive skills and creative writing at the same time, devoting time to teaching the skills necessary for analyzing comics in preparation for the analytical essay,[1] while also teaching students how to develop a story that relies on the interaction between visual and textual elements. In "Autographics: The Seeing 'I' of the Comics," Gillian Whitlock argues that students need interpretive skills derived from art and literature, and the complex visual grammar of comics requires readers to skillfully decode the relationship between the visual and the textual to deeply comprehend meaning. In order to teach students to produce rich graphic narratives, they must first become adept at the demanding task of interpretation and close reading of comics so they may transfer knowledge to make informed design decisions in their own writing. By alternating between interpretive and skill-building practices, in which weekly assignments and activities focused on close reading for one session and applied creative writing in the following session, students were able to apply comics theory to individual projects. In this way, activities and assignments prompt students to alternate between interpreting the work of professional comic artists and building their own graphic writing project.

This course relies upon a drafting process that helps students work through their ideas, getting feedback along the way. This sort of recursive writing process, a mainstay of contemporary creative-writing and composition courses, emphasizes returning to and revising work in order to improve it. Part of the goal of this course is to teach students to engage in a writing process that helps them to develop the craft of telling a story through words and pictures, with particular attention to the relationship between text and image. Because words and pictures "have to work together seamlessly enough that readers barely notice when switching from one to another" (McCloud, *Making Comics* 21), the task of writing through comics is complex and must attend to multiple layers of storytelling, including telling through words, telling through images, and telling through the relationship and placement of these elements on the page. Throughout the term, small group work and writing workshops help students draft, give and receive feedback, revise, and edit their work before finally creating a rich visual-textual story in the form of a mini comic. Weekly activities focus on helping students get to the next level of building the mini comic, with assignments built around plot development, character development, world building, and publication.

In an interdisciplinary course combining literature and design to study comics, Alison Mandaville and J. P. Avila make a case for using graphic novels to teach students to apply their learning about text, image, narrative, and design through interpretation and adaptation of a panel in Art Spiegelman's graphic novel *Maus*. In one of their assignments, students are required to interpret the visual and transform comics into a monotextual medium, which teaches visual literacy and composition skills simultaneously. Similarly, I designed a set of activities and assignments that approach writing through comics from multiple directions to help students learn through integrating the various modes of talking, writing, and drawing. Some assignments start from the oral, while others begin with the visual or the written. This approach teaches students to interpret comics from multiple perspectives and practice versatility in terms of composing. Since most students will likely have a stronger skill set in one aspect of comics composing—either writing or illustrating—activities that target both skills and integrate other modes will provide better opportunities for student learning.

Writing with students provides a way to model good writing as well as the drafting process. Throughout the course, I followed the assignments to create elements for my own comic. I created my character sheets and shared these with class. I asked for feedback and suggestions and used that opportunity to model and discuss how we can be more helpful readers and responders for each other's writing. I shared my drafts along the way and also my anxiety about how far I was (or was not) along in the writing process. I brought my final comic to the end-of-quarter student showcase and displayed my comic on the table with comics created by students.

The "teacher-writer" who models the process (and struggles) along with "student-writers" became a pedagogical norm for composition instruction in the 1970s (Eng). While the field has moved beyond the process movement, the post-process movement maintains some of the philosophical ideals of the paradigm shift to student-centered learning spaces and a destabilization of power in the classroom. According to Joseph Eng, "For some composition instructors, writing with students is a worthy and familiar practice because it answers the call for an active, committed pedagogy that encourages teachers to write frequently for both personal and professional purposes." This practice of writing with students reflects the position of the National Council of Teachers of English (NCTE), which maintains "writing teachers should themselves be writers," and the scholarly arguments by Bruce Robbins and Wendy Bishop, among others, who call for "teacher-writers" to engage themselves in the classroom.

MINI COMICS

In this course, the major creative-writing project is a mini comic in which students apply what they have learned about narrative storytelling and visual rhetoric to practice creative writing. The learning objectives for this assignment are for students to:

1. Demonstrate an understanding of the genres and history of comics and be able to situate their own work within the tradition.
2. Demonstrate proficiency analyzing both their own and peer comics to address the issues of narrative, composition, and style within stories and use that analysis to revise their own creative work.
3. Demonstrate an effective writing process in order to better understand their own strengths and weaknesses within that process.

A mini comic generally refers to a self-published comic book, photocopied or printed off at home, usually stapled in the center. Mini comics and "zines" provide writers with an inexpensive way to create and distribute their work. They are traditionally small, inexpensive, and hand-made. Commonly photocopied or printed out from one's home computer, these little booklets are usually cut, folded, and stapled together. However, mini comics are not limited to this low-tech form of production; these little stories are also produced on scrolls, folded up accordions, and sometimes bound with more ornate fasteners like ribbons or sticks and twine. For our purposes, mini comics only need to be double-sided, folded, and bound. Students have the choice of a traditional stapled comic or other forms of binding, like ribbon, glue, or rivets, and are encouraged to consider how the style of the final product reinforces the visual rhetoric of the story. For example, binding with rivets makes sense for a story situated in an industrial setting or one about robotic cats.

STORY INVENTION AND PLOT DEVELOPMENT

We begin the term by generating a list of popular types of narrative that appeal to students by looking at preferences in complementary media forms. I ask students to brainstorm about their favorite types of movies and books in order to get a sense of the stories and themes they are drawn to. Once they come up with a list of books and movies, I ask them to look for comparisons in order to identify common elements. Next, we discuss the themes and characters that exist across their favorites. We look to the list of universal themes put forth by Will Eisner in *Graphic Storytelling and Visual Narrative* so we can identify common tropes. Eisner argues that most stories fall within specific frames: stories that satisfy curiosity about little-known areas of life, provide a view of human behavior under various conditions, depict fantasies, surprise, or amuse. After using writing to brainstorm and conversation to discuss story types, we turn to examples of favorite comics and students repeat the process of listing favorites and noticing patterns. Once we identify what types of stories, genres, and artistic aesthetic we are drawn to, it is time to start creating our own.

To begin the process of story invention, I find activities that provide students with opportunities to articulate their ideas through dialogue with other writers to be especially effective. To prompt students to verbally draft and hone mini comic proposals, I use a "speed-dating" activity that requires them to describe their idea a number of times to different students while also listening to the ideas of others. This activity encourages quick, informal summaries as students rotate to new partners every two minutes, sharing their story ideas over and over. Through listening to the ideas of others, students tend to complicate their own proposals, adding story elements that resonate. The act of telling and retelling resembles the recursive writing process of drafting and revising, albeit through verbal and interpersonal communication modes. Informal speed-dating activities like this also allow for listeners to ask questions and make suggestions, allowing for an early form of peer review that informs story (re)invention.

After the speed-dating loop is complete, writing groups are formed. Using the whiteboard to make everyone's project visible, students share a quick description of their comic and write their name and the genre of their comic on the board. The next part of the activity is similar to mind mapping, in that names are linked and clustered on the board by project likeness, laying the groundwork for writing groups. Since students have already spent time discussing their projects with half of the class during the speed dating, this activity goes rather quickly, with notes on the board serving as short-hand for what they have already discussed. Many affinity groups form easily and naturally through this activity; for example, groups commonly form around the hero/heroine's journey, battles with demons, stories about alienation and not fitting in, satire, and travel.[2]

Finally, story invention moves from verbal processing to writing and visualizing narrative as students draft a one-paragraph proposal and introductory sketch. The proposal requires students to identify the genre, develop a working title, describe the setting and characters, and present the problem, conflict, or challenge the protagonist will face. The first sketch may present setting, characters, or elements of the problem. Proposals go through a peer review process in which students read proposals aloud to writing group members, make revisions based on group discussion, share revised written proposals with group members, and then make another round of revisions before submitting for credit and instructor feedback.

COLLABORATIVE COMIC DRAFTING

Since writing a story may seem daunting to many students at first, I have found that conversation is an especially effective way to begin the brainstorming and drafting process, as it helps get the stories out of students' heads and into words and images. In this activity, students work in small groups, with one person telling the story for their mini comic to their writing group while listeners interpret the story and transcribe it visually and textually. The story should have a beginning, a middle, and an end. The task of writing through comics challenges writers to juggle the demands of developing a story, visualizing that story, illustrating it, strategically using visual elements specific to comics, and creating a physical manifestation of it all.

I encourage students to turn to the framework of popular tropes like fairy tales and the hero's journey if they are not sure where to start; for example, once upon a time there was a person, they went on a journey, they faced many obstacles, they struggled and overcame obstacles, and then they lived happily ever after. While this strategy runs the risk of setting the stage for simple, formulaic story forms, using recognizable story devices can minimize anxiety that can block novice writers when the cognitive challenge is too great. The pedagogical use of templates can provide the necessary amount of scaffolding to help students deal with the "elements of the task that are initially beyond the learner's capacity, thus permitting him to concentrate upon and complete only those elements that are within his range of competence" (Wood et al. 90). The scaffold, in this case the formulaic "once upon a time" narrative structure, can be removed once the students are able to master the task at hand and eventually perform the task without it.

While one person tells their story, half the listeners write out what they hear, producing a rough script of the story, and the others draw what they hear, creating a rough storyboard. Writers and illustrators are usually unable to keep up with the storyteller, even if the storyteller is encouraged to go slowly. After the storyteller is done, writers and illustrators share their written stories and drawings, and the group discusses what key elements were captured through words and images.[3] This part of the activity helps illuminate what is most importance so writers can capitalize on these elements. Each person in the group takes a turn as the storyteller and listeners alternate between writing and illustrating.

Through telling their story to classmates, students begin the drafting process through external verbal processing. For students who prefer interpersonal learning styles, this activity can be an extremely valuable step in beginning the composition process. When students listen to the stories of their classmates and make decisions about how to articulate ideas through words and images, they practice interpretive and composition skills that prime them to develop their own creative work. In addition, this fun and informal drafting activity fosters an environment where writing groups are seen as supportive and collaborative rather than surveilling and punitive in response to one's work. After describing the story in class a number of times, through speed dating and collaborative drafting, students begin the process of composing their mini comics textually and visually. The decision whether to begin from the visual or textual is dependent on the learning objectives of the course. As this course was designed in service of a creative-writing major, the textual production was made primary with the goal of using the visual to support the written story (rather than influencing it). Alternatively, beginning with storyboarding and then moving to scripting would also provide a rich pedagogical exigence for leading with an emphasis on visual rhetoric.

SCRIPTING THE STORY

While the first telling of the story is still fresh in their minds, students have an opportunity to hone it through the process of telling it again, but this time in writing by their own hand. For this activity, students translate the story into prose form such that the written version must read like a script, explaining what the visual version will look like.[4] Similarly to scriptwriting done for film and TV, the writer needs to include language that describes elements like visual perspective and setting so the audience can imagine what the director wants the viewer to see. Scriptwriting can serve as a useful process for drafting the narrative arc before investing time visualizing the story, especially for students with less artistic experience with illustration. In the comics industry it is common for a team of writers and illustrators to collaborate on development. This means that writers need to create a script of the story, along with dialogue, so that illustrators can visualize it, and illustrators need to be able to design artwork that conveys the story as written.

FROM SCRIPTING TO STORYBOARDING

After students script their story, the next task is to begin to visualize it, imagining how to tell it through a combination of words and pictures. Drawing on the script, a visual outline of the story is created through rudimentary thumbnail illustrations with a short description attributed to each panel. This step is intended to teach students to apply the meta work of describing the story and visualizing the main scenes that anchor it, as they did when telling classmates how they envisioned the story, to writing and drawing it out.

The assignment prompt requires that thumbnails be temporally sequenced, leading the reader through the story, showing the basic script with drawings that correspond. The main task is to show readers (with images) and tell them (with words) the basic layout. Dialogue is not needed at this stage, but is encouraged if it will help readers follow the story. Throughout the term, I worked on creating my own mini comic alongside students to model the writing and feedback process, as well as encouraging students to let go of perfectionism during the drafting stage. In the example I presented, I organized my storyboard using columns to show students how to break down the meta script and create rough thumbnails to visually outline the story. Students could organize the storyboard using one column for the script and a corresponding column for the thumbnails or organize thumbnails horizontally with the script points written below or above the sketches, leading the reader through the story from left to right.

This step is not about accurately illustrating panels, but rather drafting a very rough scene to test out the feel in the context of the bigger picture. Thus, I encourage students to aim for eight, twelve, or sixteen thumbnails (since pagination of final mini comics comes in multiples of four) with the idea that these sketches can serve as the foundational images to expand upon for each page. In addition, I encourage students to use stick figures and simple shapes at this stage rather than spend too much energy on perfecting illustrations.

Thumbnails and storyboards are important writing-process tools for organizing the early conceptualizations of the visual narrative. After creating rough thumbnails, the goal is to combine words and images to create a more complex storyboard.[5] These storyboard illustrations, although still rough, need to include some detail such as all characters, dialogue, attention to perspective in the form of close-ups or long shots, and recognizable features of a setting.

After working independently, students share storyboards with writing groups to elicit feedback on overall story engagement as well as specific elements. Readers are told to consider whether dialogue and images help the reader follow the storyline and make suggestions for illustrations or dialogue that may be needed to fill in the gaps. When illustrations are confusing or unclear, group members try their hand at revisions to get it right. Next we move to elements of storytelling, and ask if the narrative arc is present. We graph out the panels in the storyboard that signal setting the scene, introduction of a problem, dealing with conflict, and the resolution. We look at the genre and consider ways to further develop the comic. If it is a comedy, does it need more humor? If it is action-oriented, do the panels convey movement? If it is a serious piece, does it make the reader think deeply? After groups meet to discuss their storyboards, I lead a discussion on how common visual devices are used to signal narrative tropes and lead readers through the story in predictable ways. We look at examples in our own work for clues, and discuss ways we might revise our own comics in the next stage based on what we have learned from each other.

Scripting and storyboarding hones creative-writing and design skills by teaching students to visualize what is written and write what they see. When these skills are brought together, rich graphic stories are possible. As students move from interpretation of other comics to creating their own, I find that activities that encourage students to develop their ideas through multiple modes increase creativity and decrease the likelihood that students will get stuck or experience writer's block. Moreover, these complementary activities can provide more visually inclined students with the opportunity to create a rough sketch of the key story elements before committing time to the finished artwork and allow more naturally artistic students to expand their storytelling through images.

Developing Characters

Comic illustrators use a variety of means to differentiate characters. One comic artist may contrast body and facial types where another may draw characters in a similar manner, but use a particular feature or icon to differentiate characters. In order to develop characters, we start with a character sheet, which prompts students to visualize characters and also develop a rich inner life for them. Character sheets require students to illustrate characters with a front, back, and side view (using the same scale for all characters), as well as describe their physical characteristics and personality, including elements like age, body type, personality traits and quirks, likes and dislikes, family and friends, and hobbies and fears, as well as give them a backstory. Students are required to develop three characters and bring character sheets to writing workshops, where we ask whether the illustrations convey a sense of who the characters are.

I supply students with a generic character sheet for drawing figures to scale, but also include links to other creative-writing character sheets available online and encourage students to draw on the categories that matter most to them. Most students rely on the categories I suggest during a mini lecture on character development, such as gender, occupation, race, and personality traits. Beyond that, students elaborate about characters in ways that align with the types of stories they are telling. For example, when the hero's journey is drawn upon, the main character's personality traits and motivations are most important, whereas slice-of-life stories that focus on interpersonal interactions benefit from elements about friends, family, and birth order, which helps readers understand characters better through relational complexities, and the inclusion of information about hometown and current place of residence is important to character development in comics that draw on the genre of the road trip. In the final version of their mini comics, some writers adapted the idea of the character sheet and created a profile page at the beginning of their narrative to introduce readers to the characters.

After reviewing the character sheets, we delve deeper during writing workshops to ask questions about characters' desires and motivations. To move beyond a simple story and complicate the narrative, we work on "the want," asking what else specific characters might say or do in specific panels on storyboards. For example, if a character has a weakness for ice cream, integrating the frozen treat into current scenes or adding panels or scenes where the character's desire for ice cream is played out can deepen character development. In a story using the theme of the heroine's journey, one might integrate a scene in which the main character makes a midnight run to the only grocery store in town to satisfy an ice-cream craving, but is met with locked doors on account of a power outage. Another scene that furthers this same theme in a satirical comic might be one in which the main character thinks she has hit the jackpot when her car is hit by an ice-cream truck only to learn the truck is completely out of ice cream.

By expanding upon characters' wants, comic writers can deepen the narrative by illustrating how characters deal with dilemmas as they move through the plot. Moreover, providing greater insight into the characters' inner life helps readers engage more deeply in the story, as they applaud the success of sympathetic characters and smugly cheer on the demise of those deemed evil.

Visualizing Expression

Another important way to develop characters is through the visual details of facial expressions and bodies in motion. To capitalize on the creativity of motivated students, I rely on collaborative comic-writing activities as well as independent creative-writing activities. Comic jams are an improvisational collaborative writing activity in which one comic is created by a number of artists, with each person drawing one panel and then passing the comic along to the next person. While the comic jam is especially effective for brainstorming narrative options, adaptations on the comic jam can make workshops more engaging as multiple people share in the creative process of developing characters.

When using comic-jam activities, there is no standard for the number of panels needed. Pedagogically, four panels provide enough opportunities to practice variations without taking too much time for a creative practice during workshop time. Each activity begins with a five-minute drawing activity in which students refer to a chart of basic comic facial expressions or bodies in motion that they can emulate. This activity can be done in the traditional comic-jam fashion with each person drawing whatever comes to mind, or in a more guided fashion, with a prompt at each rotation. For example, the second artist must draw the character with the same expression or body movement but using their own style, whereas the next artist needs to draw a different expression or body in motion as prompted by the instructor. The activity of drawing someone else's characters in an assigned position or expression forces students to draw outside of their comfort zone and practice new techniques. Alternatively, the comic jam can be adapted as a guided practice that helps students visually develop their own characters. Rather than pass their paper along to other students, in this version, students draw one of their characters in four different positions, dedicating five minutes to each drawing. After comic jams, students discuss what they intended to draw and discuss the nuance across expressions and expressive anatomy. Group members provide feedback about effectiveness of visual elements and offer suggestions when needed, often sketching out possibilities for one other. Lev Vygotsky's cognitive research, *Mind in Society*, shows that peer-based activities like this can be especially effective in helping less competent students develop skills from more skillful peers who supply just enough assistance to provide the needed "boost" to achieve a task.

WORLD BUILDING

Whereas traditional creative-writing classes dedicate attention to establishing the setting within a story, when writing through comics, developing a sense of place is called "world building." In *Making Comics*, McCloud suggests using five strategies to improve world building, specifically through the establishing shot, which gives readers a way to gain a sense of the world in which the characters live and supports a reader's connection to the characters. Extending panels to the page edge so the image "bleeds" to the edge rather than containing the image of the setting in discrete panel borders is a common trick used to give readers a sense that they are enveloped in the story world. Presenting the landscape from a low, off-center angle and focusing on the landscape by excluding dialogue, as well as increasing realistic detail and "an increase[d] sense of depth, can increase the perceived size of a setting—regardless of its size on the page" (McCloud, *Making Comics* 165).

In thinking about world building, we start with the setting and consider if there are enough visual elements to give the reader a sense of place. Using tips and strategies proposed by McCloud, and including a caption that describes it, students are prompted to create an illustration that exemplifies the setting of the comic. Students bring a hard copy of their illustration to discuss with their writing group and also post a copy on the discussion board so we can focus on a few examples, ranging from images that represent real places to fantastical worlds, integrating world-building strategies effectively for whole-class discussion in the writing workshop.

During this phase, students comment on their design choices and how the strategies utilized enhance the setting they are attempting to create. Combining the real and the fantastic, one student played with the fourth wall to show readers they were looking at a manufactured world. Her world reflected a thoughtful application of the reading she presented about world building in the comic *The Punisher* by Gregg Rucka, where she noted, "there is no dialogue. As a reader, we are only able to observe the actions and environment. As McCloud states, the silence of the scene allows us to 'step off the twin conveyor belts of plot and dialogue' in order to wander about the scene." Similarly, the setting she created was devoid of dialogue, giving the reader a sense of what it was like in her main character's home— an everyday apartment full of the usual furnishings, with the exception of a closet used for sleeping in. In her magical forest-glade illustration, another student applied the concept of the bleed to her setting and described the efficacy of how "the bleed effect allows the background to appear open and endless, despite the limited space actually provided to the picture itself." In an establishing shot of a library, a third student used bleed and one-point perspective to focus on an increased sense of depth.

Visualizing Time

Visualizing the flow of time through comics writing is a complex process because time is conveyed within panels, as well as in the space between them (the gutters). Strategic use of panel borders, dialogue, sound effects, and other visual elements allows comic writers to pace the story with intentionality. In order to teach this aspect of comics writing, students are required to identify a scene that would benefit from attention to time and focus on visual and textual components to develop this part of their comic.

Dialogue can be strategically used within one panel to convey a sense of time as moving, even though a single panel reflects a particular moment that is relatively static. At the basic level, panels move the reader through time, with dialogue focused on one character at a time in one panel at a time. A more nuanced way in which the passage of real time is represented is through a single panel that shows multiple people talking at once, with speech bubbles leading readers through time via each person's speech. A panel that contains multiple characters speaking can also be used to slow down time and depict a shared moment. Narrative time is not only conveyed within panels, but through the space between them as well. Panels and people may be spaced close together or far apart to convey time. By placing panels close together, the reader gets the sense that the story is moving quickly.

One way in which the passage of time is depicted in comics is by breaking down a scene into multiple panels and making small changes to each panel, similar to a string of time-lapse photos. To illustrate this point, I created a set of illustrations of the main character from my comic to show how time passes. In one set of four panels, to show the character falling asleep, I drew a close-up shot that focused on his eyes, with his eyelids closing a little bit more in each panel to show how small changes within the panel can control a sense of time. Additionally, when the amount of space between panels (or gutters) is increased, so is the sense of time, as the eye takes more time to get from one element to another. To demonstrate how time can be slowed down (or sped up) through gutter manipulation with the same sequence of panels, the same images of a sleeping monster are presented, albeit with a wider gutter. In students' final comics, they used similar techniques to visualize time. In a road-trip comic, the illustrator manipulated elements across a sequence of four panels that showed a van driving all day. In these panels, a van and the sun are the visual elements that are slightly manipulated in each panel, with the sun moving along its arc from high in the sky to nearing the horizon while the van progressively drives further out of the line of sight with each panel. In a comic that relied heavily on themes of time, the illustrator used iconic imagery of the minute hand of a clock moving from one minute to the next in each panel. In addition to traditional visual elements, she manipulated words visually, placing text boxes underneath each panel and sandwiching words between ellipses to force the reader to slow down as they read that "everybody's. . .|. . .time. . .|. . .runs out." In a comic depicting a hero's journey, time was shown to move slowly both within and across panels, as well as through spacious gutters. In the first panel the main character was shown as walking through the desert and time that had already passed was depicted with each footstep visible in the sand behind him. In the following panels, we see the character from a variety of angles as he contemplates his situation. The shift in perspective gives readers a chance to slow down and think, as if from another angle, in the same way the character does. Finally, the amount of white space within and between panels further adds to a sense of stillness that is quite different from busy and tightly packed panels.

The most nuanced form of presenting the passage of time is achieved through negative space and a lack of imagery. In the space between panels, "the producer gestures to the textual referent via the text and the consumer 'does or makes' the referent by the process that McCloud defines as 'closure'" (Bolling and Smith 42), which is a "phenomenon of observing the parts but perceiving the whole" (McCloud, *Understanding Comics* 63–66). It is easily understood as the reader mentally fills in the gaps of what happens during the time between panels. In her piece "Autographics," Gillian Whitlock argues that students need interpretive skills derived from art and literature:

> The vocabulary of comics represents figures and objects across a wide iconic range from the abstraction of cartooning to realism; its grammar is based on panels, frames, and gutters that translate time and space onto the page in black and white; and balloons both enclose speech and convey the character of sound and emotion. This grammar makes extraordinary demands on the reader to produce closure. (968)

To demonstrate this effect, I used a sequence of panels that show a mother running to the door and opening it to check on her son who had just woken from a bad dream in a previous scene. In the first two panels the mother is running towards the door, a little closer to the door in the second panel. In the third panel, readers only see her hand reaching for the doorknob, and in the final panel, she is holding the door open and speaking to her son. The reader does not need to see multiple panels of the door in the process of opening to understand what is happening. Rather, the reader is able to infer what the missing panels are and cognitively fill in the gaps of what is happening in a story. In this way, the space between the gutters serves as yet another visual cue to reference the passing of time.

Final comics created by students demonstrated how closure can be created in a variety of ways. In a comic about a mermaid chasing a star, closure across pages can be seen as readers make sense of what happens between the image of the mermaid staring longingly at the star floating above her head on one page and the point at which she holds the star in her hand in the next panel, which also happens to be on the next page. The virtual gutter that is created by the binding between pages serves as the imagined space where readers infer that the mermaid reached up to catch a star, even though there are no images showing her arms in motion as they reach up and grasp it. In a horror comic in which a family member is secretly a demon, a series of three panels use inference and closure to reveal the killer. In the first panel, readers see a smiling grandmother, followed by a girl standing with a noose in front of her face in the second panel. In the final panel, readers reach the climax of the story when they see the girl's body hanging from the rope while a demonic version of her grandmother—complete with devil's horns, sharp teeth, bat wings, and a pitchfork—is flying in the air and laughing. Readers do not need to see the grandmother transform to recognize that she has become the demon, because there are enough visual cues to signal that this is the same person. The smiling grandmother and the demon have the same facial structure, as well as the iconic symbols used to represent elderly women—eye glasses and hair pulled back in a bun. Nor do readers need to see panels that show the process of the hanging to realize the noose eventually went around the girl's neck and her grandmother did the hanging. Strategic lack of imagery provides suspense while visuals of the grandmother, the girl facing the noose, a hanging body, and the laughing, demonic grandmother provide the closure necessary to tell the whole story.

Production

Mini comics come in a variety of shapes and sizes, with the most common format created using standard sheets of paper, folding, and stapling. An eight-page 5.5″ × 8.5″ booklet can be made from two sheets of standard-sized paper folded in half on the long end, or an 8.5″ × 11″ booklet can be created the same way from 11″ × 17″ legal-sized paper. For those who like to get twice as many pages from the same amount of paper, they can cut the sheet in half as well as folding it, such that a sixteen-page 4.25″ × 5.5″

booklet can be created from two sheets of standard paper and a 5.5″ × 8.5″ booklet can be made from legal size. Another popular size and shape is the twelve-page 5.5″ × 5.6″ virtually square booklet created from one double-sided sheet of legal paper organized into sixths by folding down the center and cutting it into thirds. In Europe the term "small press comic" is synonymous with mini-comic publications measuring A6 (105 mm × 148 mm) or less. A multitude of options exists in terms of shape, size, and materials and students were free to choose the format that seemed most fitting to their comic.

Although there are many variations on complex pagination, the assignment required students to produce at least eight pages to meet the minimum requirement for a "B" and at least twelve pages for an "A" (regardless of the number of panels within pages). For the book-binding process, students had the option to use an old-school cut and paste process or take a new-media approach. Those sticking to low-tech means of production cut and pasted panels or pages onto master sheets and then created double-sided photocopies of pages in binding order. The process of making mini comics is relatively easy, but it can be a bit confusing when it comes to organizing and printing pages, because they are not sequential until they are combined into a booklet. In order to ensure comics came out in the correct order, a thumbnail dummy book and a draft of the final booklet were incorporated as part of the draft process.

Those opting for high-tech production chose from a variety of software options and inserted images into a document, organizing pages using the template for double-sided book binding. Although some programs, like Microsoft Word and Pages, can be finicky about positioning images, they allow students to insert copies of their images into a document and move them around easily. The other benefit of traditional word-processing software is that these are programs with which students are already familiar so the learning curve is low. More robust programs like Adobe InDesign and Publisher offer more professional options, but these are not free and universities may not have subscriptions to them in computer labs. There are also free comic-building programs online.

In line with material practices in the comics community, students made copies of their comics to share and distribute widely. Our class participated in a campus-wide student showcase at the end of the term, where students displayed the mini comics to the university community at large. Students were welcome to share, sell, or give away their finished projects. Since our university fosters a strong commitment to community engagement, students were also encouraged to share their comics in the world beyond our classroom and campus by promoting their creative writing through the local comic-book store[6] and local comic conventions.[7]

CONCLUSION

Engaging students with comics in creative-writing courses has significant implications for today's students, as it provides opportunities to teach students to think critically about texts that are part of their everyday lives and which are often considered benign. When I asked students why they enrolled in this class, the majority said it sounded "fun," a comment I never hear with my 100- and 200-level required composition courses. By the end of the course, students were saying it was fun to create and read comics, but also a lot of work. From a teaching and learning perspective, using texts students perceive as "fun" can counter motivation issues faced in courses where students are uninterested or resistant to reading the texts.

While most students perceived this course to be "fun," it was not without its challenges. In terms of student learning, a handful of students did not have any background in drawing and expressed concern that they would not be able to illustrate a mini comic. I encouraged novice illustrators to rely on simple shapes or stick figures; the learning goals for the course do not focus on the aesthetics of art, but rather the ability to write a story with words and images. In most cases, novice illustrators either opted for simple drawings and/or spent more time learning to draw their main characters, and worked with them in more complex ways.

Throughout the term, we discussed how the experience of analyzing and writing comics is transferable to careers beyond college. Storyboarding is used in marketing and advertising. The integration of art, and more recently animation, into stories is important to report writing, journalism, and public relations work. To help students situate their own comic writing, they wrote an artist statement and a reflection about how their mini comic fit within the larger tradition in terms of content and style. This reflection served as a tool that could be used for a portfolio, as well as demonstrating learning within the specific course. In addition, a field trip to our local comics store was used to give students a view of the business side of the comics publishing market. Using comics in the writing classroom can improve learning and has the benefit of preparing students for careers beyond college when explicitly taught.

Notes

1. The critical analysis essay is one of the major assignments in this course, requiring students to practice applying theoretical skills of close reading while placing themselves within an academic conversation in the field of Comics Studies.
2. To deal with the evolving writing process (as well as absenteeism), groups are reorganized as needed to make workshop time productive.
3. For groups large enough to have two writers and/or illustrators, there is an opportunity to compare and contrast what elements stood out in the story.
4. Prior to asking students to write a script for their own mini comic, one can practice this meta-level writing skill with sample comics as well. Such an activity would ask students to bring in a favorite comic and write out a script for a section of the text.
5. Students were given the option to go beyond pen and paper to experiment with online storyboarding programs such as Pixton and Storyboard That. A few mentioned trying digital programs, but found the learning curve too intensive during our ten-week quarter system.
6. In the middle of the term, our class took a field trip to the local comic-book store and the owner talked to students about the options for publishing, promoting, and selling their comics, and encouraged them to contribute to the local comics section, which a number of them did.
7. After our course ended, a number of programs across campus got together to get a table at the annual GeekGirlCon, which, at the time of writing, a number of students from this course were scheduled to participate in.

Works Cited

Aune, M. G. "Teaching the Graphic Travel Narrative." *Teaching the Graphic Novel,* edited by Stephen E. Tabachnick, Modern Language Association of America, 2009, pp. 223–229.

Bishop, Wendy. "Places to Stand: The Reflective Writer-Teacher-Writer in Composition." *College Composition and Communication,* vol. 51, no. 1, Sept 1999, pp. 9–31.

Bolling, Ben, and Matthew J. Smith. *It Happens at Comic-Con: Ethnographic Essays on a Pop Culture Phenomenon.* McFarland, 2014.

Dong, Lan. *Teaching Comics and Graphic Narratives: Essays on Theory, Strategy and Practice.* McFarland, 2012.

Eisner, Will. *Graphic Storytelling and Visual Narrative.* W. W. Norton & Company, 2008.

Eng, Joseph. "Teachers as Writers and Students as Writers: Writing, Publishing, and Monday-Morning Agendas." *The Writing Instructor,* Aug 2002, http://www.writinginstructor.org/eng-2002-08

Hammond, Heidi Kay. "Graphic Novels and Multimodal Literacy: A Reader Response Study." *University of Minnesota*, 2009, www.conservancy.umn.edu

Jacobs, Dale. "More than Words: Comics as a Means of Teaching Multiple Literacies." *The English Journal,* vol. 96, no. 3, Jan 2007, pp. 19–25.

Kojima, Hiroyuki, Shin Togami, and Ltd Becom Co. *The Manga Guide to Calculus.* No Starch Press, 2009.

Losh, Elizabeth, Jonathan Alexander, Kevin Cannon, and Zander Cannon. *Understanding Rhetoric: A Graphic Guide to Writing.* Bedford/St. Martin's, 2013.

Macdonald, Katharine Polak. "Batman Returns (to Class): Graphic Narratives and the Syncretic Classroom." *Teaching Comics and Graphic Narratives: Essays on Theory, Strategy and Practice,* edited by Lan Dong, McFarland, 2012, pp. 221–231.

Mandaville, Alison, and J. P. Avila. "It's a Word! It's a Picture! It's Comics! Interdisciplinary Approaches to Teaching Comics." *Teaching the Graphic Novel,* edited by Stephen E. Tabachnik, Modern Language Association, 2009, pp. 245–253.

McCloud, Scott. *Making Comics: Storytelling Secrets of Comics, Manga and Graphic Novels.* William Morrow Paperbacks, 2006.

———. *Reinventing Comics: How Imagination and Technology Are Revolutionizing an Art Form.* William Morrow Paperbacks, 2000.

———. *Understanding Comics: The Invisible Art.* William Morrow Paperbacks, 1994.

National Council of Teachers of English. "Teaching Composition: A Position Statement." NCTE, 18 Aug. 2008, http://www.ncte.org/positions/statements/teachingcomposition

Nitta, Hideo, Keita Takatsu, and Ltd Trend-Pro Co. *The Manga Guide to Physics.* No Starch Press, 2009.

Robbins, Bruce. "It's Not That Simple: Some Teachers as Writers." *English Journal,* vol. 81, no. 4, Apr 1992, pp. 72–74.

Sousanis, Nick. *Unflattening.* Harvard University Press, 2015.

Tiemensma, Leone. "Visual Literacy: To Comics or Not to Comics? Promoting Literacy Using Comics." *World Library and Information Congress: 75th IFLA General Conference and Council,* 2009, www.ifla.org/past-wlic/2009/94-tiemensma-en.pdf

University of Washington Tacoma. "SIAS Mission, Vision and Values | UW Tacoma." University of Washington Tacoma, 2014, www.tacoma.uw.edu/chancellor/mission-values-and-vision

———. "Writing Studies." University of Washington Tacoma, 2016, www.tacoma.uw.edu/sias/cac/twrt

Vygotsky, L. S. *Mind in Society: The Development of Higher Psychological Processes.* Revised edition, edited by Michael Cole, Vera John-Steiner, Sylvia Scribner, and Ellen Souberman, Harvard University Press, 1978.

Whitlock, Gillian. "Autographics: The Seeing 'I' of the Comics." *MFS Modern Fiction Studies* vol. 52, no.4, Winter 2006, pp. 965–979.

Wood, David, Jerome S. Bruner, and Gail Ross. "The Role of Tutoring in Problem Solving*." *Journal of Child Psychology and Psychiatry*, vol. 17, no. 2, Apr 1976, pp. 89–100.

PART II

Graphic Novels in the Literature Classroom

Teaching the History and Theory of American Comics: 20th-Century Graphic Novels as a Complex Literary Genre

Lauren E. Perry

My specialized Expository Writing course approaches American graphic novels (and/or comics) in the form of a literature survey course, with special attention paid to comic theory and the composition of graphic narratives. The foundational weeks of lecture begin with research and survey of book and print culture, similar to how students learn print culture while studying bibliography. The critical component of learning about the historical construction of what we now refer to as graphic novels is instrumental in allowing students to discuss several critically important graphic novels from the 20th-century. The course introduces the scientific process of reading various styles of graphic narrative so that students develop confidence in their ability to perform close reading on very complex graphic texts. Understanding the complex interplay between signs (language) and image-signs, along with paneling construction and artistic choices, is akin to studying diction and style in non-graphic literature. After the initial first two weeks of historical background, allowing all students in the course to feel competent in their ability to discuss texts in the proper historical context, students proceed to read a selection of graphic texts from across genres. The course texts do not move chronologically, but begin with comics from the

L.E. Perry (✉)
University of New Mexico, Albuquerque, NM, USA

© The Author(s) 2018
A. Burger (ed.), *Teaching Graphic Novels in the English Classroom*,
DOI 10.1007/978-3-319-63459-3_5

69

Underground Comix movement so as to introduce close reading with what are arguably the most thematic texts. Each course text is paired with in-depth study of the author(s) and artist(s), historical context, and video pairings of interviews and the like. This multimodal approach to a literature survey yields critical analysis of what students initially see as flat texts. So often, due to the enormity and instability of the field in the academic perspective, comic history and science are ignored while the texts themselves get interjected into regular literature courses. The underlying objective of this course is for students to see that graphic narratives are more complex than traditional literature. The combination of theoretical inquiry into the graphic text reading process, historical context, and survey of varied graphic texts allows for students to get a very strong footing in a field where it is quite easy to feel overwhelmed and unsure of any real competency due to such high volumes of texts. The pedagogical rationale and methodology of teaching graphic novels in this way has been emphatically effective in getting students to engage with, research, and close-read graphic texts as literary works and, ideally, as texts with the potentiality for more complex readings. The course promotes literary readings of, but also critical thinking about, why graphic texts are more than literature because of a dual narrative capability.

Teaching graphic novels, like teaching any literary genre, is daunting due to the kinds of choices one has to make about scope, perspective, and course texts. It is important for literature professors to be one step ahead of their students, to not be so deeply familiar with and ingrained in a text that they cannot teach it in hopes of new insights. I try to choose different key texts every semester, but one thing has never changed about my approach to teaching this course: I do not ask my students if comics are literature because throughout the semester we establish that comics are actually much more complex than literature and grow out of an entirely egalitarian print tradition. Though some scholars would argue this question of being literary no longer holds sway, Hillary Chute's 2008 article asks in its very title "Comics as Literature?" The question certainly lurks in the background of my students' minds: are comics "literature" or literary? My approach aims at affirming not just that comics/graphic narratives are indeed literary but that their literary potential quite possibly exceeds that of narratives without images.

No doubt students are aware that comics without literary value exist and sell at high volumes. The best example of decidedly non-literary comics are companion comics that retell the plots of superhero films. Their plots, their transitions, their very artwork are created in order to promote the film and hardly stand alone. Texts studied in this course are meant to offset and disprove the fallacy that comics only serve to convey narratives that either already exist primarily in the physical world or are for those whose reading capabilities are less evolved. Students are aware that the average person on the street would answer "no" to the question of comics as literature (a response that often corresponds increasingly with age). They probably have parents and relatives who would insist the answer is no. In my class time and throughout the duration of the course my goal is to mute the power of this question in order to make room for much bigger questions and subsequent answers through critical thinking and analysis: What constitutes a graphic narrative? What is the effect of reading an image alongside text? Can text become an image? What is an image-sign? How do we read graphic narratives differently than a series of symbols or icons? This course provides an entrance into the genre through which students feel equipped to analyze and respond to graphic narratives as complexly literary while highlighting what makes the genre unique using comics terminology and theory.

This specific course recently won an award as the best specialized section of non-genre Expository Writing course. The University of New Mexico's Expository Writing courses (English 220) are for sophomores after they've passed English 110 and 120 (basic composition courses). The shared Student Learning Outcomes are to:

1. Analyze Rhetorical Situation: Students will analyze the subject, purpose, audience, and constraints that influence and determine what kind of document (genre) they will write.
2. Find and Evaluate Information: Students will develop research strategies for their rhetorical situation, and then gather information from primary and secondary sources; they will evaluate the source for quality, validity, and appropriateness for the rhetorical situation.
3. Compose Documents: Students will develop strategies for generating content, organizing it into a logical structure, and otherwise shaping it to address the needs of their audience within particular disciplines. Students will design written and multimodal documents.
4. Present Documents: Students will edit and revise their writing to provide clear meaning and coherent structure; they will use effective document and paragraph structure, documentation and genre conventions,

and document and multimodal design to create a rhetorically complete presentation.

5. Reflection: In reflecting on major writing assignments, students will be able to explain course outcomes and how they have achieved them.

These outcomes are met organically within the parameters of the writing course through students' response writings and in-class writing. Instructors (mostly graduate students) adapt this course in a variety of ways. Expository Writing aims to hone students' writing skills in specialized sections from which they can choose. Currently, there are sections on the Southwest, Medieval Quests, Rap and Hip Hop, Short Stories, and several others. Teaching graphic novels as Expository Writing has required refocusing the skeletal set of terms away from literary study toward sophomore-level writing and analytical skills. The assignments have retained their value in an Expository Writing course because they require analysis and the successful communication of complicated ideas which depend on concise writing. One of the course outcomes of the University of New Mexico's Expository Writing courses is for students to produce a certain quantity of writing. Writing about graphic novels is a new challenge for most students. Explaining what they observe as working (or perhaps not working) in narratives, utilizing both images and text, requires them to think about writing while also helping them understand the texts.

METHODOLOGY

This course allots considerable time to introducing comic history, theory, and print culture. To allow students to engage in what might be very unfamiliar territory, my overall approach is to teach them the basic history of 20th-century comics first. Most students, even those who read comics for pleasure, are new to basic comic history. Beginning with the pulps, the four-color printing press, radio, and population shifts in urban areas, the history of comics clearly begins well before Superman's inception in May 1938. Tying in the history of print culture also allows students to see the medium as being truly different from traditional literary/printed texts in form beyond questions of style.

My academic interests in graphic narratives lie in the mental process of comic reading. Comics are a unique medium where the potentiality of multiple narratives is pressured and demonstrated. In my own work, I rely heavily on Ferdinand de Saussure and semiotics in studying what Hannah

Miodrag calls *image-signs* and *image-in-series*. Asking students to view language as constructed from the unit of the sign (signifier and signified) allows us to draw connections between iconography and signs. Being critical of language enables students to push on the idea that language and image are separate. I like to use the example of a stop sign. Is the word STOP not part of that image? At what point does a sign become an image? I also lecture on the arbitrary nature of signs, and ask students the difference between the word "chair" as an arbitrary signifier and my rudimentary (read: terrible) drawing of a chair. Discussing comics as vastly complex literary texts requires that students begin with a shared understanding of this new "language" of comics. Image and language's intersection evokes questions of multiple, convergent, and divergent narratives all working at once, which texts like Scott McCloud's help students unpack. Works like Neil Gaiman's *Sandman Chronicles*, in which multiple artists render protagonists in disparate ways, have been the focus of my most recent presentations. I assert that text/word bubbles become images. How we read the two in conversation while reading graphic novels is what I find fascinating.

Though I do not explicitly teach semiotics or more advanced literary theories that I see in play in graphic narratives, these concepts provide a skeletal framework for discussion questions I pose to the class. Students have a knack for answering profound questions I have not gone so far as to ask. They understand theory without my explicating it and their genuine observations are very valuable and usually quite complex. Most of them are not English majors and their observations about the hybridity of image-signs and language often unearths ideas I cannot teach. Echoing McCloud, they observe key parts of language and iconography at work, but perceive a whole that tallies with their individualized reading experiences. Such is one of the great rewards of teaching: seeing students respond in fresh and more advanced ways than expected.

COURSE TEXTS

I choose course texts representative of the micro-genres of graphic novels and what illustrates (pun intended) innovation, what has changed the trajectory of the medium, and what will subvert student expectations of graphic narratives. The explanation that follows of the course progression through the various texts in sequence provides rationale for the order and for the selection of these specific texts. I often swap out similar texts for one another (Frank Miller's *The Dark Knight Returns* for *Year One*, for example). Each time I do, the results are slightly different but seem to be nonetheless valuable to students. As I will address in the assessment section, a large portion of the students' grades comes from response writings. With the relatively high number of individual course texts, I do not require response writings on every text. Students may decide not to write about or respond to a text they do not understand or that, for whatever reason, is indigestible to them.

Putting as many of the texts as possible on reserve at the library is also conscientious in that these texts can be expensive and are often unavailable (through campus bookstores) as used copies. Local comic shops also appreciate it when I phone my semester's text list in to them so they can have copies on hand, and they almost always offer students a discount. Visiting comic shops allows students to get a feel for the culture of the industry, which we address when we get to texts like Harvey Pekar's *American Splendor*. That being said, the internet allows students to obtain unauthorized PDF files of comics. I don't care how they get them, so long as they read and come prepared to class. I insist they get to know their classmates and exchange information, so that if sharing is a necessity, it can be communicated and achieved. Comics should not be an exclusive realm accessible only to the privileged, from Cap to Iron Man to Alison Bechdel's *Fun Home*.

My classroom must be open and inviting to newcomers and that begins with making sure all students have access to the course texts. Comics, with their history rooted in dime novels, penny dreadfuls, and the pulps, are the site of collective learning. From their inception, these texts were meant to reach all, to exclude none, and to convey underrepresented voices and narratives. Comics were meant for everyone and especially those willing to put aside apprehension about being judged as low-class. Comics employed the underdogs and were produced for the everyman and child. My classroom imitates this historic sentiment by reproducing it. Comics are to be shared, exchanged, and discussed. To ignore this past and not fully realize it is to lob comics in with the classist, racist, elitist tradition of other forms of literary works. They are not novels. They are something else, both through their propensity for complexity and through their historic foundation. Students participate in this almost unwittingly. They enact what comics capitalized on: the desire to tell great stories at little cost for whoever wanted to listen.

I have started the semester in teaching this course with two different texts, both of which I will admit sound like unlikely choices because they are non-literary and non-academic. My most frequent choice has been to lead with Grant Morrison's *Supergods*. The alternative is *Superheroes!: Capes, Cowls, and the Creation of Comic Book Culture* by Laurence Maslon and Michael Kantor. I usually prefer Morrison's text for several reasons. It is a lively, entertaining accompaniment to in-class historical lectures. Morrison is also one of the most renowned living comic writers. His breakdown of the Golden, Silver, and Bronze Age of comics, though profanity-laden, is valuable in that his perspective is from someone working inside the industry. It also sets the tone for the course in a way. Though my personal pedagogy is one that utilizes humor to draw students into conversation, I am well aware that many courses take a more solemn approach to the teaching of comics. I want students to feel comfortable discussing this medium. Morrison's voice as a writer does a great deal to establish that this industry is fun, unique, special, and exciting, but also artful. Morrison is more than a bit eccentric, but overall a trustworthy, credible, informed source on a subject that matters to him a great deal. Maslon and Kantor's text is also a great introductory work in that its exploration and explanation of the relationship of pulps and radio to comics was instrumental in the development of the comic world as we know it today. A bit less entertaining but erring much more on the side of the factual, I tend to choose *Superheroes!* over *Supergods* when I have more advanced students. I should also note that I keep a running list of suggested texts on our course website. This list is helpful for students who finish our course texts and seek more points of reference. It is also a great tool when students begin choosing their final paper topics and Canon Proposal texts. The Canon Proposal is a scaffolded assignment which lends itself to the final research paper topic. Students choose and present on a graphic text, arguing for its place in an imaginary graphic novels "canon," answering a variety of questions about how and why it deserves canonization. Regardless of the text I choose, we view Grant Morrison's website, his interviews, and a photo to prove that one of the comic greats looks like a Scottish Lex Luthor. Humor is key for breaking down apprehension.

Both of these texts establish the Golden Age of Comics, the Silver Age, the Bronze Age, and the Underground Comix movement. Though neither is exhaustive, the rationale for leading with either of these texts is to allow students to understand the scope of our course's conversation. Inevitably, questions arise about comics older than the 20th century and/or comics in other countries. These are points when the list of suggested reading comes into play, as there are many other texts for the student most interested in newspaper strip comics, or French political cartoons, or another specialized genre or style. The internet enables showing short strips of various works in class at a moment's notice. We study Fredric Wertham's 1954 treatise *Seduction of the Innocent* and the court cases that followed, ultimately resulting in the Comics Code of Authority. Even under the self-regulated Code, comics repurposed themselves in the Silver Age, and again with the bucking of the Code in the Bronze Age. When equipped with an understanding of the historical pressures on this particular form of print production, students are capable of seeing that these texts do not exist in a vacuum but are, like other literature, very much a reproduction of and reaction to their respective time periods and current issues. Again, the internet fills in much of the historical foundation and visuals needed to provide an accurate scope of the evolution of comics in early 20th-century America.

After spending the first two weeks establishing the foundations of graphic narratives and their connections to history and print culture, the next step is to acquaint students with the graphic novel format itself. Up until this point students will not have discussed literary qualities in class, but from this point forward the aim of the course is to examine how language and images work together in each specific text. Discussions on content, style, and form evolve naturally into discussions of theme, voice, and literary analysis. The most profitable result of teaching the course as front-loaded with the historical and theoretical contexts is that students organically begin discussing the texts unquestionably as literature. I attribute this to students feeling knowledgeable enough to discuss comics because they can see a framework. Most students in a more traditional literature survey course have at least a vague conception of the world history of literature and/or know of at least a few canonical authors. On some level, they all know that Shakespeare's plays differ greatly from a beach read. With comics, that is not the case. Many students are solely familiar with superhero comics and frequently believe comics are a relatively new phenomenon. Dispelling these misconceptions and demystifying the origins of comics helps students move toward discussing the actual narratives. The approach is inverted from that of the standard literature survey course where students accept canonical literature as being literary because it inherently "is."

In this course students are not required to think of literature or what constitutes the literary nature of texts at all until they are equipped with the historical and theoretical knowledge and terminology to talk about how comics are created in the most basic sense. Simplifying how comics are "made" and how they have been created in this small scope of American history allows for a somewhat fresh perspective on what is being created and how. Though we do not address comic theory until after the first two course texts, we do address basic graphic novel terminology like panels, gutters, word bubbles, and lettering, and these enter into discussion about our first course text directly from our lectures and discussions on the history of American comics.

The first graphic novel we read is Art Spiegelman's *Maus*, for several reasons. As Daniel Worden writes, "It is no surprise, given comics studies' justified interest in legitimating comics as an artistic medium, that Art Spiegelman's *Maus* remains the centerpiece of comics studies, the subject of many of the first academic essays about comics to appear in literary studies journals and books published by university presses" (60). *Maus* might seem a predictable choice but, while there are always a couple of students who have encountered the text previously, by and large the majority of college sophomores have not read *Maus*. They are always already familiar with the topic of the Holocaust, as most have read *The Diary of Anne Frank*. In reading *Maus*, the subject matter becomes secondary to how the narrative works to convey a genre with which they are familiar. Students simultaneously study and discuss one of the most important foundational graphic novels while also honing their scholarly voice about the differences between telling a Holocaust memoir through graphic narrative and through a more traditional text.

Maus also works to dispel several misconceptions students may have. Students' response to the hands-on reading of a graphic novel in totality expands upon the groundwork laid by earlier readings. Many of the students in these 220 courses have never read a graphic novel, and the importance of their first reading of a complete narrative in graphic form cannot be overstated. I emphasize the importance of the reading process and participation because of how it differs from other mediums. These first discussions are critical in their foundational revelations of the potentiality of differences from person to person. Some give primacy to the written narrative while others give artwork their focal attention. *Maus* establishes the possibility that comics can convey thematic material in a way that does not trivialize the subject matter. We discuss the effect of seeing animated mice being hung in the streets, what we know they represent, and that *Maus* is a true story. Being forced to envision brutal violence in our own minds is more graphic than any drawing could be. *Maus* also establishes that color is not necessary for an impactful graphic narrative. Millennial students are primed by the flash and pageantry of CGI Marvel movies and the husky-voiced Christian Bale. Many respond to *Maus* with very real surprise at how effectively black and white works for Spiegelman's purpose. Lastly, *Maus* (being the 1992 Pulitzer Prize winner it is) silently illustrates a point I make to them early on in the course: that superhero comics are by no means the only comics. Though superhero comics allowed the medium to flourish in early 20th-century America, it is because of the Underground Comix movement that artists and writers began producing for an adult audience. Our course would not exist were it not for works like *Maus*.

From *Maus* we move to Harvey Pekar's *American Splendor*. I usually use *The American Splendor Anthology* as it is an excellent example of what a comic looks like when it is serialized and drawn by several different artists. Coming straight from Spiegelman's mostly linear narrative, which is completely his own art and text, students are often unsure what to think of *American Splendor*. The connection between *Maus* and *American Splendor* is the portrayal of human existence. From the anxiety of creating a nonfiction Holocaust memoir to the banalities of lower-middle-class life in Cleveland, these texts are united in their clear connection to the freedoms of expression created by the Underground Comix movement of the 1980s. *American Splendor* addresses social issues representative of working-class Americans of the late 20th century. What makes teaching *American Splendor* worthwhile is its historical gravitas and the fact that Paul Giamatti's 2003 film of the same name not only tells Harvey Pekar's story, but includes interviews with the writer himself. Hearing Pekar's accounts of his personal history as a comics author puts the material of what many students describe as obscure humor (or even depressing content absent of all humor) into context. Hearing the author speak makes the strips come alive in a way no lecture from a professor could achieve. Though admittedly there are always students that just don't "get" the humor, the majority of them come out thoroughly enjoying it and responding well to the themes and style. This is an instance where a multimodal, technologically-enhanced approach makes all the difference. We spend three to four class periods on this text (at least one more than we do on other texts) and the difference in response from the first class meeting after they have read the text in isolation versus reading the text after watching the film is stark. Enabling students to connect reality to what is being presented in the comic allows them to understand why Pekar's work matters. If art is the perpetual endeavor to convey human emotion and the human condition, *American Splendor* re-emphasizes the capability of comics to be part of the artistic realm.

The next course text is Scott McCloud's *Understanding Comics*. Students have just come off of two black and white Underground Comix and moving into this complex, dense work of comic theory is a welcome change. I choose to incorporate McCloud later in the course so that students can observe what McCloud explicates. At this point in the semester, students have a shared bank of knowledge and references from which to draw. We spend a considerable amount of time discussing comic panel transitions and how McCloud's concept of "closure" constitutes the majority of comic reading. As a class, we look back to *Maus* and *American Splendor* to examine how they utilize the pieces of McCloud's various theories and explanations. I often accompany McCloud's text with reading quizzes and explain *Understanding Comics* as the textbook for comic theory. McCloud's text also does the pivotal work of establishing the history of comics long before and far outside the tiny scope of our course. He references Egyptian hieroglyphics, European comics, and Manga, and provides extensive graphs of information on the differences among comics across cultures. I emphasize repeatedly the importance of understanding that comics are in no way a uniquely American phenomenon. Other cultures' comics are not only widely read but widely influential across time and literature. I have had guest professors lecture on Manga and political comics, as they are not my area of expertise. I feel it is always good form to let someone else speak to students throughout the semester.

In addition to treating comics as more of a science, McCloud's choices in his own work greatly impact student thinking about the potential of comics. Students dissect why McCloud chose to write this seminal work of comic theory in comic form, often in their response writings for this text. They quickly notice and are receptive to his use of comic form to emphasize and illustrate (pun intended) his main ideas. For example, students especially love an instance in McCloud's definition of closure where he explains over the course of three panels how readers assume his legs are present even though they cannot see them. The humor lies in the realization triggered by McCloud's stating that his legs are not there due to the panels being a comic representation (61). Students recognize the meta nature of proving theory about comics through the use of comics. The impact of McCloud's work cannot be overstated in its importance to the evolution of an adult readership's attitude toward comics. The same can be said about his work in its importance to helping novice literature students approach comics. It provides terminology, clarifies the graphic narrative reading process, and traces the tradition of using images and text in unison cross-culturally and across history while proving that serious content can be conveyed using comics.

Once students have digested McCloud and are comfortable using more technical terminology, we transition back into narrative texts. Students have now experienced three very different uses of black and white as a stylistic choice. The next selection is Frank Miller's *Sin City: The Hard Goodbye*. I choose *The Hard Goodbye* because of the themes it presents (clearly defined ideologies and their perversions) and because of several specific panels in which the inversion of black and white, including negative space and lining, makes for very complex art. Miller's influence in the comic world cannot be overstated and in the event I have not chosen *The Dark Knight Returns* and/or *Year One* as one of our course texts, *Sin City* presents the opportunity to lecture on Frank Miller (albeit briefly). We watch interviews that explain his influence on *Batman* and *Daredevil* comics. We also watch the film adaptation Robert Rodriguez and Miller co-directed in 2005. We examine *Sin City* as a film noir/Raymond Chandler-esque graphic novel which lends itself nicely to a mini lesson about the film noir genre. The film adaptation of *Sin City* is remarkable in that it is word-for-word and nearly panel-to-panel faithful to Miller's original work. Students witness the direct translation from graphic narrative to screen and their analysis of what is lost, changed, bettered, or suffers is critical. With the exception of comic enthusiasts in the course, viewing the film creates for the students the first instance where they have read the graphic novel prior to viewing the film. Most have seen many of the Marvel films, Spider-Man, or Batman adaptations but have not read the texts. *Sin City* is old enough that even some of the comic readers are new to the adaptation and moreover unacquainted with seeing a translation that is so direct. The responses often divide the class into those who prefer the text over the film and vice versa. Regardless of their opinions of *Sin City* itself, this juxtaposition further allows students to explain in detail how the images and text combine to make a thematic, dense narrative in comic form, as well as in comparison to film.

The following course text is *Batman: The Long Halloween* by Jeph Loeb and Tim Sale. This is the course's first color text (color only appears briefly in the *Sin City* film adaptations, one of the few points of departure from the text) and uses muted blues, greens, greys, and purples. It is unlike any of the existing Batman films in that it, too, is written in the style of film noir. Students know Batman from films, but usually not as the detective character so clearly influenced by characters like Sir Arthur Conan Doyle's Sherlock Holmes. The print style and formatting also provide an example of what a graphic novel looks like when it is a compiled edition of many serialized prints. *The Long Halloween* was published in issues coinciding with holidays from 1996 into 1997. As the origin of Harvey Dent, many students make connections between the text and Christopher Nolan's 2008 film *The Dark Knight*. *The Long Halloween* is also the course's first superhero comic. Students find it to be much different than the flashy, vibrant look of the film industry's billion-dollar marketing campaigns. Loeb and Sale's text reads more like a Raymond Chandler novel than a box-office smash. This iteration of Batman is highly stylized; his cape is almost its own character. Students use the skills they've acquired from analyzing complex works like *Maus* and *American Splendor*, together with the terminology and theory from McCloud, to produce complex panel-to-panel close readings.

The course's first Batman text is followed by none other than the Man of Steel in Mark Millar's *Superman: Red Son*. This text demonstrates the profound complexities of graphic narrative storytelling and its ability to critique ideologies through well-known characters. *Red Son* is a perfect example of innovative lettering, word bubbles, retroactive continuity (or ret-con), and Infinite Earths. Most students are familiar with Superman as a symbol of inherent Americanness. Millar (a Scot) uses Superman's altered origin story as a tool to critique conceptions of government power, class, and national identity. The clarity and seemingly overt gesture the text makes by turning Superman into a Soviet is friendly to students new to these critical concepts. These are often sensitive topics in that students are undoubtedly informed by their parents, backgrounds, social groups, and popular culture about politics, religion, and the economy. Writing about critiques is daunting. *Red Son* is consistently the top choice for students' Canon Proposal presentations. Once they have participated in critical discussion of the themes present in *Red Son* they are apt to explicate why Millar's unique take on Superman is literary. They engage in the reading of Millar's critique with excitement while witnessing that, although the world of comics can be daunting to enter, it only takes one writer or artist to change how we view the limitations or potential of a character. Because they respond so well to the narrative itself, getting students to write in detail about how and why *Red Son* works is a fruitful exercise. It also allows for a broader critical discussion of concepts like ideology and power, which again reinforces the complexity of comics written for an adult readership.

Each course text successively subverts one genre misconception or expectation at a time. *Maus* establishes the potential of comics, *American Splendor* the dark humor, *Understanding Comics* the scientific, historical cornerstone, *Sin City* the perversity and complexity of art, and *The Long Halloween* and *Red Son* the negation of the belief that all superhero comics are mindless and cheaply cinematic. Other texts I have taught in other offerings of this course are *Saga*, *The Sandman Chronicles*, and *Persepolis*. The course texts are all somewhat interchangeable but I do strongly believe that the ordering of texts based on their styles, themes, and relationship to one another works exceptionally well for college students. Teaching the texts in conversation with one another creates points of reference and a clear connection between vastly different texts. Students learn that reading comics is a highly participatory, involved, demanding process.

Assessment

The primary mode of assessment in this course is the response writing assignment. Introduced on the first day of the class, students are given a semester schedule in which there are roughly ten response writing due dates corresponding to the schedule of course texts. I assign as many as eight but no fewer than five of their choosing, which are due on specified dates. I set a number of responses that must be submitted over the course of the semester. All responses engage the same basic prompt. This promotes a sense of scholarly freedom, alleviating and preventing arbitrary or lackluster responses to texts that students might not connect with, and promotes self-efficacy. Aside from semantics like page length and formatting, the only stipulations are that students must make a meaningful connection to the graphic text from their own perspectives as scholars. No summary or assigning of value is allowed without extensive analysis. Being that the instructor has read each text, summary results in points lost as it is unnecessary to valuable response writing. I do tell students that a profitable writing exercise might be to begin by summarizing what they see happening in form, style, or narrative, and from there see what connections they naturally begin forming, but to then delete the summary aspect of the document as these are usually short writing exercises. By making the required page length short, students are challenged to condense their ideas. Connections must be made in concise writing and students learn the valuable skill of discarding writing that is unnecessary or does not answer any part of the given prompt.

Another allotted portion of the students' grade in this course is the Canon Proposal. At this juncture, I teach the problematic nature of any canon, who compiles it, and how, historically, canons have excluded minority voices. We define the difference between what is literature and what is literary. I question how emerging fields like comics trouble the very idea of comics as literature when they are clearly something more and from a very disparate origin. Despite the irony, students theorize and speculate about the assignment's title but nevertheless create this imagined "canon." It is a chance for revisionist inclusion in what "should" be read based on what is literary. I have had students complete this assignment in presentation form, written paper form, and as a combination of both. All have worked equally well in getting students to consider the problematic nature of any canon and at the same time challenge themselves to externalize and verbalize what they see as distinctly literary in these graphic texts. As Daniel Worden explains, "Canonization, then, can pose just as many problems for scholars and students interested in comics as a form or medium as it does to produce a sense of intellectual legitimacy" (60). What works truly "belong" in the canon? The assignment tasks students with envisioning the call for canon proposals by, say, the Library of Congress, in which requests must be presented to include certain works in a canon display of graphic novels. For this assignment, students must first choose a text. They can select a course text, a text from the list of suggested reading, or a text they locate on their own so long as I approve it by a certain date prior to the Canon Proposal submission deadline. Proposals must situate the work historically and explain the text's innovations, style, themes, and importance to other works. The result is a clear explication of what makes the work unique and why it is indeed literature. The results of this assignment are best when made into presentation form. Requiring students to use visuals (Prezi, PowerPoint, or simply Google Images) when presenting about an explicitly visual subject promotes close reading of panels and attention to detail that otherwise goes unachieved. The presentations are timed. The assignment also works well as the initial phase of their argumentative research papers. My personal pedagogy rests on student-centered and student-driven investigation. By allowing students to choose a text that interests them for the analysis and close reading necessitated by the Canon Proposal, these assignments often highlight issues worth researching and arguing in their final project.

The final research paper, though not as critical to students' grades as the response writings, is the culmination of the semester's work. A standard argumentative research paper assignment, the only thing that makes this assignment unique to this course is that I must allow for a wide array of sources. Though there is absolutely ample scholarly, peer-reviewed work on texts like *Maus*, students' investigation of research questions about new(er) superhero comics do not often find the same quality sources. I emphasize the importance of audience when explaining allowances made for less-than-scholarly sources. Students know they are writing to me as their audience: someone friendly to those new to comics but also someone well-versed in geekdom. If a source doesn't sound viable to them or is not written by someone with apt qualifications, students may either email me a link to run the source by me, or better yet, use their judgment. I let them know that if I would discount the source, they should as well. Students may write about any aspect of the text they choose. The most important requirements of the assignment prompt and rubric are those requiring close reading, analysis, and close attention to what the graphic narrative conveys, no matter the perspective from which these are approached.

Closing Thoughts

This course is a favorite of mine to teach because of the responses of students at the completion of the semester. Course evaluations are always overwhelmingly positive, superlative even, and reflect excitement at having learned a great deal in one semester. Students consistently convey feeling able to approach the texts without apprehension. Put bluntly, students end this course understanding comics and a variety of subgenres on an advanced level. They produce inquisitive, thoughtful, critical-thinking responses that simultaneously help them become better writers by being challenged to explain a new kind of text. It is remarkable how students teach us about our own fields without meaning to, and that is repeatedly what I receive through student responses and papers. Fresh eyes see texts in nuanced ways and make connections I would not have made. This course's inclusive nature brings many students to the discussion that would otherwise have forgone the opportunity to study a genre and medium so often rife with misconceptions. They participate in the social, communal quality of comics that makes them accessible. They use literary analysis skills to read these texts for complexity of form and content. As comics continue to evolve and readership expands, this course will evolve and find new ways to reach students through new combinations of texts. Teaching comics as a medium that is literary through its history will continue to change as new comics are produced that create different conversations.

Works Cited

Chute, Hillary. "Comics As Literature? Reading Graphic Narrative." *PMLA: Publications of the Modern Language Association of America,* vol. 123, no. 2, 2008, pp. 452–465.

Eisner, Will. *Comics and Sequential Art: Principles and Practices from the Legendary Cartoonist.* W.W. Norton, 2008.

Howe, Sean. *Marvel Comics: The Untold Story.* Harper, 2012.

Loeb, Jeph., Tim Sale, and Bob Kane. *Batman: The Long Halloween.* DC Comics, 2011.

Maslon, Laurence, and Michael Kantor. *Superheroes!: Capes, Cowls, and the Creation of Comic Book Culture.* Crown Archetype, 2013.

McCloud, Scott. *Understanding Comics: The Invisible Art.* Harper Perennial, 1994.

Miller, Frank. *Sin City: The Hard Goodbye.* 3rd ed., Dark Horse Books, 2010. Print.

Miodrag, Hannah. *Comics and Language: Reimagining Critical Discourse on the Form.* University Press of Mississippi, 2013.

Morrison, Grant. *Supergods: What Masked Vigilantes, Miraculous Mutants, and a Sun God from Smallville Can Teach Us About Being Human.* Spiegel & Grau, 2011.

Pekar, Harvey. *The New American Splendor Anthology.* Four Walls Eight Windows, 1991.

Spiegelman, Art. *The Complete Maus.* Pantheon, 1996.

Worden, Daniel. "The Politics of Comics: Popular Modernism, Abstraction, and Experimentation." *Literature Compass,* vol. 12, no. 2, 2015, pp. 59–71.

CHAPTER 6

"What Is the Use of a Book … Without Pictures or Conversations?": Incorporating the Graphic Novel into the University Curriculum

Alison Halsall

In *Alternative Comics*, Charles Hatfield zeroes in on the complex nature of the medium, arguing that "Comics are challenging (and highly teachable) because they offer a form of reading that resists coherence, a form at once seductively visual and radically fragmented. Comic art is a mixed form, and reading comics a tension-filled experience" (xiii). The graphic novel is a relatively new medium of visual literature that is in the process of being justified as both a serious art form and an effective teaching tool, much as the children's picturebook experienced almost thirty years ago.[1] Kimberley Reynolds notes that the suspicion and disdain with which 20th- and 21st-century parents, educators, and librarians can still react to graphic novels is similar to the responses to "penny dreadfuls" and "penny bloods" in the 19th century (65). In spite of the suspicion and disdain, or even the damning by faint praise that some graphic novels have inspired among "serious" critics, this new and "vibrant form of literary publishing" (Baetens and Frey 4) deserves more analysis in terms of its serviceability in the university and college classroom. As I see it, the graphic novel medium is wonderfully complex and

A. Halsall (✉)
York University, Toronto, ON, Canada

© The Author(s) 2018
A. Burger (ed.), *Teaching Graphic Novels in the English Classroom,*
DOI 10.1007/978-3-319-63459-3_6

entirely appropriate as a learning tool in the university and college curriculum at all levels of study, both undergraduate and graduate. Among many things, it enables a student and reader to deepen her or his abilities to understand visual codes of rhetoric, the complex codes of narrative, and to comprehend how these two levels of reading animate one another. A graphic novel requires active reading on a student's part in terms of making sense of word and image, frame and frame, and assembling all of this fragmented knowledge into a longer, coherent narrative. This exciting intermediality of images and texts also points to the omnipresence of the visual in contemporary culture. In our increasingly visual world, visual literacy and comprehension are crucial parts of communication. As Nancy Frey and Douglas Fisher point out, elements of literacy, such as reading, writing, speaking, and listening are regularly taught in the classroom, with little recognition given to the act of viewing (1). The graphic novel thus represents a unique learning tool that allows university and college students to hone their skills at "reading" images, to study the interanimation of texts and images, and to produce rich analyses and communications about them.

The graphic novel is a medium I regularly employ in my university classes, from first to fourth year. It is an extremely effective tool in facilitating the transition pedagogy currently used in liberal arts programs. This transition pedagogy is a guiding philosophy that scaffolds and mediates the first-year learning experience in order to promote student success. In the first year, for example, a graphic novel can help students move past the feeling of intimidation that comes with being in a university English or General Education classroom, especially if they are taking an English or Humanities course to fulfill an academic degree requirement. Students perceive graphic novels to be more accessible, current, and fun to read, and therefore do not dread them the way they might canonical literature. Getting students excited about the act of reading by means of a visual text goes a long way in terms of encouraging students to deepen their interest in literature in general, as I discover in my pairing of selections from Homer's *Odyssey* and Frank Miller's *300* in my first-year General Education English class, which explores "The Literary Imagination." By beginning this course with the literary epic, one of the very oldest literary forms, my class initiates its discussions about literary imaginings, as *The Odyssey* imagines and reimagines the adventures of the famous hero Odysseus in the course of his return from the Trojan War to his kingdom of Ithaca. From Homer's poetic text we examine some visual representations of his characters (in painting and pottery), and then move into an exploration of Frank Miller's graphic novel *300* to see how these characters have been transformed, yet again, in the present day. As contemporary adaptations of *The Iliad* and *The Odyssey* prove, these figures from Ancient Greece—first imagined by Homer and his group of bards—have become the subject matter for visual imaginings and reimaginings ever since. In the same first-year General Education English class, Art Spiegelman's *Maus* saga, narrating the history of his family's experiences as Polish Jews during World War II, provokes thoughtful exchanges about the politics of representation, the writing of history and memoir, and the concept of survival. For the four weeks leading up to this text, we examine how poets and playwrights imagine people. We take a look at Geoffrey Chaucer's wonderfully vibrant character the Wife of Bath through her prologue and tale. We then turn to Robert Browning's dramatic monologues ("My Last Duchess" and "Porphyria's Lover") to see how some particularly psychotic perspectives are represented in poetic form. Shakespeare's *Othello* allows us to examine how the complicated issues of race and gender were imagined in Elizabethan times. Finally, with Spiegelman's *Maus*, we examine a visual-literary text that imagines war and the peoples affected by the war. Invariably, my students are profoundly affected by this important visual text, and come to class energized by their reading experience and eager to share their thoughts about it.

In a second- and third-year university class, a graphic novel such as Alan Moore's *The League of Extraordinary Gentlemen* again introduces students to a kind of reading experience that they initially *perceive* to be less formal or rigorous, but which actually demands a surprising amount of literary knowledge and visual literacy on their part. Situated at the end of my unit on the Victorians in my third-year Humanities course on adaptation, Moore's *League* allows students to visualize representations of the 19th century while also learning about the practice of intertextuality, as well as the modes of satire and parody. We read this graphic novel after three or four weeks spent contextualizing the paradoxes of the Victorian period (by means of poems, short stories, and paintings) in an effort to understand the nostalgia for Victorian literary and artistic forms that still informs our contemporary period.

By the fourth year of the undergraduate experience students are generally equipped to specialize, to synthesize deeper, more theoretical readings, and to read texts that operate at the word/image level in a more sophisticated fashion. In my fourth-year English course on "Literature and the Other Arts," Frank Miller's *Batman: The Dark Knight Returns* and Alan Moore's *V for Vendetta* inspire productive discussions about politics, the media, and the ethics of the hero/superhero. *Batman* is an excellent graphic text to finish with in our exploration of adaptations between and among literature, film, visual art, and music. It is primarily thanks to the numerous versions of the Batman story that circulate in popular culture, specifically the current franchises and campy 1960s television series, that so many of my students are familiar with, at the very least, something about the Batman myth—his secret identity, the names of his city and his lair, his sidekick, and his enemies. As we discuss, *Batman* is a story that is always in circulation, and in turn is a story that is influenced by the stories—both literary and visual—around it. Many of the key elements of the Batman myth stem from visual art and cinema, as we explore. Creator Bob Kane's original concept for the Batman came from a Leonardo da Vinci sketch of a man wearing bat-like wings, and Kane's other sources include Bela Lugosi's *Dracula* (Browning, 1931) and Douglas Fairbanks' performance in *The Mark of Zorro* (Niblo, 1920). Gotham City was modeled on the city of film noir (seen in *The Maltese Falcon*), 1930s gangster movies, and 20th-century crime fiction. As students come to realize, Miller "borrows" some of the conventions from pre-existing Batman texts in an effort to produce his own, unique, and distinctly literary-visual "take" on the Batman myth. Following our analysis of *Batman: The Dark Knight Returns*, we examine Alan Moore's graphic novel *V for Vendetta*. Both graphic novels share a fascination with the modern or post-modern city, as well as the principles of government and the systems of surveillance that control this dystopian urban jungle. In our exploration of the modern-day superhero (like Batman and Superman), we circle back to earlier discussions we had in the course about Odysseus, the hero in our ancient epic, *The Odyssey*, to investigate the nature of the villain. Is V a hero or a villain (or both)? What about Batman and Superman: are they heroes or villains? As we discuss, *V for Vendetta* and *Batman: The Dark Knight Returns* blur the polarization of good and evil in their creation of heroes (or anti-heroes, as the case may be) with particular causes, whether it is V's rebellion against Fascism in 1992 England, or Batman's vendetta against the Conservative Right in America. The graphic nature of these two graphic novels is what I would argue makes these sophisticated concepts accessible to university and college students who might not necessarily be familiar with these ideas already.

In short, I employ graphic novels at all levels of the university curriculum, continuously inspired by the passionate responses I receive from all types of students. As Jacquelyn McTaggart writes: "Teachers use graphic novels because they *enable* the struggling reader, *motivate* the reluctant one, and *challenge* the high-level learner" (McTaggart 32, emphasis original).

A graphic novel provokes questions and discussions about canonicity, propaganda, accessibility, and applicability at all levels and stages of learning, and most importantly, motivates students to continue to read.

More to the point, a graphic novel has wonderful potential to appeal to university or college students, addressing issues that are very topical for them, like history (*Maus, Louis Riel*), politics (*Palestine, Persepolis*), social issues (*Skim, Black Hole*), crises and personal growth (*Fun Home, Blankets, I Never Liked You*), myth and fantasy (*The Sandman, Dark Knight, Watchmen*), and so on. Once we turn our attention to this type of intermedial text, students' eyes light up and they begin to participate more passionately in lecture and tutorial discussions. This medium is already very familiar to them, not simply in terms of its subject matter but also in terms of the way it requires a reader and student to read. "The act of reading a comic cuts much more closely to how our students today receive information," Rocco Versaci writes. "I'm thinking particularly of the Internet, where the sites that I see my students visiting regularly are densely packed and ask readers to move their eyes diagonally and up and down in addition to side to side—the same kind of movements that come with reading comic book panels and pages" (Versaci 97). As a "sight-based medium" (McCloud 202), a graphic novel contains the literary hook as well as the visual imagery that seem to be increasingly necessary among contemporary young readers, and this "combination of text and graphics enhances readers' ability to understand abstract concepts in new ways" (Allison 75). A graphic novel, it seems, speaks to students on a personal and individual level. They do not begin reading a graphic novel from the position of insecurity that canonical literature provokes in them. In addition, the art does not set them apart from the text. Instead, it guides them in further, asking them to respond to the text emotionally. This emotional connection "to the art, story, or characters—is a key to visual literacy" (6), as Ryan Novak writes. This emotional connection translates into participation in class and, ideally, investment in the course concepts. As such, I find that a graphic novel is an equalizing rather than divisive teaching tool—it is a text that students have opinions about and are inspired to analyze more deeply in their course assignments.

Due to its inherently visual nature, the graphic novel also speaks to the many students who are affected by the film and entertainment industry, and different media platforms in general. Thanks to the omnipresence of superheroes in recent film adaptations (the *X-Men, Avengers, Batman*, and *Superman* franchises, for example), these adaptations help draw students' interest from the movies back into literature, and at the very least deepen their comfort level with visual texts. In my first-year and fourth-year classes, the graphic novel medium allows me to address more general topics like adaptation and transmedia storytelling, the telling of stories across multiple media platforms. Ours is an age of sampling, adaptation, and reinvention, and these superhero adaptations and graphic novel adaptations of texts like Neil Gaiman's *Coraline* and *The Graveyard Book*, for example, examine these stories as but one part of a "convergence culture," as Henry Jenkins calls it, whereby stories transform across different media platforms (in film, television, popular music, computer games, websites, toys, amusement park rides, books, newspapers, magazines, and comics).

As previously mentioned, I teach Frank Miller's graphic novel *300* at the end of my unit on the epic genre, in my first-year General Education English class. In the organization of class modules, I employ an "augmental approach" (50), to use James Bucky Carter's term, because I use a graphic novel to increase the *kinds* of texts that students in my classroom can sample. A graphic novel, in this case, is given equal billing with a canonical classic (Homer's *Odyssey*), and with other visual artifacts like film, painting, and even ceramics. Beginning the unit with selections from Homer's *Odyssey* to explore the structural and thematic features that define the ancient genre of the literary epic, our unit eventually demonstrates how these principles are self-consciously invoked in Frank Miller's adaptation of the Battle of Thermopylae. We read selections from *The Odyssey* (focusing on such characters as Odysseus, Penelope, Telemachos, Agamemnon, Athene, and Circe) alongside visual representations of these characters on classical pots and urns, all the way up to 19th- and early 20th-century paintings (by John William Waterhouse and Herbert James Draper). Our discussions about the principles of representation and adaptation that these urns and paintings feature help set the stage for our examination of Miller's *300* and its reimagining of the epic narrative in graphic novel form. Miller's *300* allows my students (who are not necessarily all English majors) to continue our discussions about the signature elements of the epic—such storytelling as the larger-than-life heroes and villains, the quest motif, and the importance placed on hospitality—and the typical narrative devices that are found in one of the oldest literary genres, tropes like embedded narratives, lists, fixed epithets, and epic similes.

300 is a text that is extremely resonant in youth culture, thanks to Zack Snyder's 2006 film adaptation, a film we screen after reading Miller's text. This augmental progression of text demonstrates the effective transmedia that *The Odyssey* and *300* are involved in, and emphasizes the cultural importance and omnipresence of Homer in contemporary popular culture to students who would not necessarily have ever even thought of this classical writer and who are more familiar with the Spartan warrior ideal displayed and parodied in popular YouTube videos. Moreover, as a text situated early in the course, *300* allows us, by means of the power of the visual, to begin our discussions about homosociality and heteronormativity, not to mention the construction of race, which we continue throughout the year. Sometimes, a graphic novel adaptation of a canonical text inspires students to deepen their connection with the source text, as occurs in my pairing of *The Odyssey* and *300*. Character archetypes and narrative patterns from *The Odyssey* and *300* crop up in our discussions for the rest of the year. And, thrilling for me to learn, students return to Homer's *Odyssey* again and again in their assignments.[2] A graphic novel thus possesses a crossover ability to inspire deep and passionate responses from readers in the reading of canonical classics.

More specifically, a graphic novel provides a more sensory and immersive reading experience, allowing students to fall into the narrative more immediately. They don't usually need to be urged to read it; instead, students are attracted by its applicability and relevance to their lived existence. Art Spiegelman's *In the Shadow of No Towers* presents a thought-provoking way into the personal and collective trauma of 9/11 that invariably stimulates much discussion among students. Spiegelman's Pulitzer Prize-winning *Maus*, though, affects students profoundly at all levels of the university and college experience, not simply because of its shocking and deeply personal subject matter, but also through its ability to render visual the horrors of the Holocaust. *Maus* inherits the special problem all Holocaust literature has to deal with when it tries to confront this historical catastrophe: how can any mode of representation—literary, cinematic, visual—do justice to what happened in the Holocaust? Isn't any representation going to fall short in the face of such horror? Spiegelman's masterpiece tackles this problem of representation and the ethics of representation through its unconventional medium: the graphic novel. Traditionally, students have approached this historical event by means of textbooks, films, and documentaries; Spiegelman exploits the graphic novel medium to unsettle the reader and force her or him to experience the subject matter in a completely new way. In Scott McCloud's terms, the universality of the cartoon is what invites so many readers (and students) into the cartoon world: "The more cartoony a face is, for instance, the more people it could be said to describe" (31). Indeed, the ostensibly simple lines in Spiegelman's graphic novel invite my first-year students to see themselves in Artie (perhaps, even, in Vladek), and the empathy they feel, and even the anger the painfully human Artie and Vladek provoke among them, keep students reading and thinking deeply about the impact of this historical event.

One of the many powerful elements of *Maus* is its extremely personal response to the Holocaust, and its involvement in survivor's guilt, on at least two levels. Vladek feels guilty for having survived the concentration camps, and Artie carries the guilt of being the son of a survivor and another survivor (his mother) who eventually kills herself. In this graphic novel Artie talks about responsibility on so many different levels, and his own personal struggles with the responsibility of representing this world event are depicted in visual form. The inclusion of visually rendered historical artifacts like photographs, maps, and diagrams, and the busyness of the visuals, encourage active reading among students and develop their skill at "reading" and decoding images. More to the point, these visual images hold a powerful place in helping to convey difficult and horrifying concepts, as I realize when we discuss disturbing frames like the hanging sequence in Volume One or even the "Prisoner on the Hell Planet" comic that Spiegelman includes to contextualize his own struggle with depression and despair. *Maus* encourages students to immerse themselves in the reading of history and invites them to speculate about how they themselves would have responded had they been faced with similar circumstances. *Maus* affects students on a visceral and intellectual level. It provokes opinions. It inspires discussion. This graphic novel transforms historical event into lived reality, and invariably encourages students to make connections to current events in the world. *Maus* is also a text that allows us to consider the graphic novel as material artifact. We discuss the paratextual apparatus that prefaces and ends Volume One of Spiegelman's story. The packaging of the story—the title and subtitle, cover art, epigraph, tragic dedication, and the dust jacket—is as much a part of the visual rhetoric the text employs as the subject matter itself. Students often overlook this paratextual apparatus, and so *Maus* is a very useful tool with which to discuss how all of these elements are as important for contextualizing the story as the story proper.

The visual packaging of the narrative invariably deepens into a discussion about the generic classification of Spiegelman's story. The intermedial form of word and image allows students to think about the hybrid literary forms the text invokes, its combination of novel, documentary, history, and memoir into a graphic novel. When encouraged to think about why Spiegelman mixes so many different genres, students move toward the realization that the visual form of the narrative signals the realization that one narrative genre alone simply cannot do the subject justice. The Holocaust and its horrors are incapable of being addressed in one genre, Spiegelman suggests. *Maus* is therefore about the personal burden of this project, and the visual nature of the text (especially the frame in Volume Two in which Artie is drawing over a pile of corpses fresh from the gas chambers) makes this point very clearly. Of course, Spiegelman's visual form also highlights the allegorical level his text operates on through his depiction of Jews as mice, Poles as pigs, Germans as cats, and Americans as dogs. By means of the visual, students are guided to think more deeply about this use of allegory: Why use different animals to represent race? What does that element add to the narrative? Does it undercut the argument that the graphic novel as a whole is making? On the one hand, discussion points to the distancing of history this allegory performs by depicting the characters as cute animals. On the other, it suggests visually that race is not reducible to one characteristic or another. There are good mice and bad mice, as we see, good pigs and bad, good and evil cats. Just as the Jews "passed" or pretended to be Poles or Germans to survive, the novel plays with its own allegory, presenting humans wearing mouse masks or mice wearing pig masks. In this visual allegory, Spiegelman playfully represents the Jews as the vermin Hitler characterized them as in the graphic novel's epigraph, ironically appropriating and undercutting Hitler's racist rhetoric.

As I appreciate on a daily basis in the classroom, and as Stephen Tabachnick notes in the introduction to his collection about teaching the graphic novel, "graphic novels fit students' sensibilities at a deep cognitive level" (4), since the intermedial textual-visual experience of reading is the new "normal" for readers and students, thanks to the Internet, PowerPoint, cell phone screens, illustrations, and photographs that bombard them in the media (ibid.). The visual is undeniably a very powerful teaching tool, as Lewis Carroll's Alice suggests by her question "What is the use of a book without pictures or conversations?" (9) when she peeps into her sister's book at the beginning of *Alice's Adventures in Wonderland*. Simply put, visuals inspire responses and students are amazingly perceptive about *what* they see. When I project a slide of a painting, an artifact, a comic strip, or a segment of a graphic novel on the screen, we spend on average between fifteen and twenty minutes "unpacking" the visual. Even without previous experience of discussing this type of visual narrative, students have surprisingly resourceful toolboxes for this analysis. In large part due to their intensely visual world, students are already attuned to questions of layout, the impact of color and organization of the image, and size. They can frequently intuit from the visual text the argument(s) the artist is attempting to make. Some of the questions we ask ourselves when looking at visuals include: Why did the creator of this image choose to depict this particular image in the first place? Why did the creator frame it in this way? What is the mood of the image? Does the image reflect a personal value system? Does it communicate ideology?[3] These questions encourage students to consider the rhetoric that is always involved in word-image combinations. The ability to decode images is a learned behavior, then, and the graphic novel allows students to refine their analytical approaches to the narrative involved in a visualization. They also learn to reflect on the context that shapes the narrative and the cultural assumptions inherent in the visual. David Lewis talks of the "synergy" (36) of picturebooks that I think can be quite usefully applied to graphic novels; he explains that "The words are brought to life by the pictures and the pictures by the words, but this is only possible in the experience of reading" (Lewis 55). Like Lewis, I firmly believe that the student brings the text to life. I'm thrilled when students leave class with an ability to think critically about the visuals that surround them on a daily basis, and with an enthusiasm for texts and new media they may not have come in contact with before.

Frequently, this learning experience includes myself, as the instructor. What often occurs in looking at a visual narrative together is that students will point to a detail or segment of the narrative that I may have overlooked, and the classroom transforms into a community of learners who are working collaboratively toward the development of knowledge and skills. Indeed, a graphic novel invites a dialoguing back and forth between and among students and teacher, one that breaks down hierarchical boundaries, and facilitates a communal learning experience. This approach produces a classroom in which active learning takes place, a classroom that is student-centered and, most importantly, one that has switched from an Instruction paradigm to a Learning paradigm. In this type of classroom instructors create "environments and experiences" that allow students to "discover and construct knowledge for themselves" (Barr and Tagg 15). These active learning methods lead to a better understanding of the course and equip students to be problem solvers and critical thinkers long after they graduate, better able to apply their learning in their daily and professional lives, and to be lifelong learners (Michael 159). This communal learning experience that the examination of a graphic novel inspires also gives students who participate immediate feedback from the instructor leading the discussion, and results in deeper learning and their increased engagement with the course material.

If *Maus* allows students to explore the allegorical mode by means of the visual, a graphic novel like Alan Moore's *The League of Extraordinary Gentlemen* allows students to see the principle and practice of intertextuality at work in a text, the interconnections between and among literary texts, and literary movements as they relate to the politics of interpretation. As I have already mentioned, students read this graphic novel at the end of a unit on the Victorian period, a unit that, according to my augmental approach, requires students to read a range of poetic texts from Christina Rossetti, Alfred Tennyson, Robert Browning, and Elizabeth Barrett Browning to reflect on the politics of gender, race, and class in the 19th century, as well as the concepts of "progress," Empire, and evolution. Robert Louis Stevenson's novella *The Strange Case of Dr. Jekyll and Mr. Hyde* is also a text they must read to consider the Gothic and the urban in the Victorian age. Another class meeting is spent on Victorian medievalism to see how the Victorians (the Pre-Raphaelite artists, specifically) appropriated literary figures from Thomas Malory's *Le Morte d'Arthur* for their art. All of these texts set the stage for this graphic novel, which requires an attentive reader to appreciate Moore's intertextual in-jokes. For example, Moore's text borrows popular ideas of Victorian identity and femininity, well-known literary characters (Captain Nemo, Mina Harker, Dr. Jekyll/Mr. Hyde, the Invisible Man), and particular literary forms (sensation and Gothic novel) to parody ideas of the socially conservative Victorian period. These characters and tropes rendered visually allow students to appreciate the practice of intertextuality that Moore models in his graphic novel.

Together with artist Kevin O'Neill, Moore fashions a graphic novel that also revels in the commercial and artistic possibilities offered by 19th-century commercial artifacts. In this way, the Victorian artifacts in front of, during, and after the story proper set the Victorian stage by commodifying it and showing how it is a commodity that a reader buys, something with which contemporary students are already very familiar. Moore's graphic novel includes games or interactive activities for its readers, like instructions on how to make Nemo's Nautilus from paper or a paint-by-numbers of Dorian Gray, to reflect further on the commercialization of the avant-garde Moore is parodying. I draw students' attention to the way each issue ends with a descriptor of what lies ahead in the next issue to talk about the practice of serialization the Victorian age developed, which is quite similar to the serialized writing with which students are familiar through fan fiction and even gaming communities. *The League of Extraordinary Gentlemen* thus immerses students in the Victorian experience, not simply through the story itself, but also through its artwork. And, in the process, Moore's graphic novel allows students to "access" this past historical period that, for many, is so far removed from their lived experience as to be easily dismissed. Even with a text as challenging as this one, I find McTaggart's claim that graphic novels "*enable* the struggling reader, *motivate* the reluctant one, and *challenge* the high-level learner" (32, emphasis original) to be quite true. There is something for every type of learner in Moore's graphic novel. All of the intertexts only widen the parameters of the text and encourage students to participate in discovering how all of these elements fit together.

But what is the larger purpose of these literary and visual intertexts to the Victorian period? How might they speak to a contemporary student? It is the concept of the superhero that provides the most immediate parallel for students. As Douglas Wolk explains, Moore is interested in "already-famous characters" because "they answer readers' needs to understand their own culture and experience" (232). Heroes and superheroes certainly speak to students on a personal and individual level, and they elicit strong opinions. Superhero narratives surround students on all sides in popular culture, and so a graphic novel about Leonidas (*300*) or a Victorian Justice League is more familiar to them than, say, Charles Dickens' *Hard Times* or Joseph Conrad's *Heart of Darkness*. By means of the superhero or hero narrative, students make connections to the world around them, from discussions about immigration (*Superman*) to prejudice (*X-Men*). Ryan Novak agrees: "Just as the Greeks once did, we too use tales of gods and goddesses as one way [sic] understand the world around us. The only difference is that our gods and goddesses wear tights and have superpowers. Superheroes function as a modern mythology, and the characters often reflect different parts of our culture and help explain so much about ourselves" (8). The heroes from Moore's graphic novel are a far cry from the vigilante values of Batman or the nationalist ideals of Superman or Captain America. In fashioning his unusual league from characters from 19th-century popular Gothic and fantasy fiction, Moore not only asks his educated readers to consider Victorian concepts of gender and race, colonialism, imperialism, and Darwinism, but also asks them to think more deeply and more generally about his ironic use of the concept of superheroism. What types of hero or superhero do students require in our contemporary moment? What does this signal to us about our needs in the 21st century? Moore's "parade of curiosities," in this way, provokes much interesting analysis on the part of students about their needs in popular culture.

Finally, as an educator, one of the attributes I appreciate most in Alan Moore's graphic novels (and, indeed, graphic novels in general) is their encouragement of active reading on the part of readers (and students), and their invitation to read and reread texts (both visual and literary). This practice of reading and rereading was brought home to me in my third-year Humanities class when one of my students complained to me how challenging she found Alan Moore's *V for Vendetta* to read. Yet she transformed that challenge into something more productive when she revealed to me that she had read it six or seven times before she "understood it." This revelation might not seem very encouraging at first glance, but when I also learned from students in the same class that they could not get through Jane Austen's *Pride and Prejudice* even once because of the "old English" it employs, the fact that this student was motivated enough to return to the same graphic text six or seven times in an effort to "understand" it, inspired me. Thus, even a text like *V for Vendetta*, which is highly complex in terms of its historical context (Thatcher's governmental policies) and philosophical viewpoints (totalitarianism and atheism), proves my point that a graphic novel is a "highly teachable" medium (Hatfield xiii), one that is certainly challenging to read, but also topical and interesting, sensory and immersive. McTaggart agrees: "The comic-book industry keeps its finger on the pulse of what is happening in the world, what kids view as 'cool,' and they respond to it with lightning speed. The industry's reward is more sales; society's reward is more student readers" (29). Reading, and the deep critical thinking encouraged by the graphic novel, is what education and post-secondary education are all about, isn't it?

I feel a similar excitement about this new medium that David Lewis once felt for picturebooks. Like Lewis, I argue that the graphic novel makes use of a complex and "[heterogeneous] form" (Lewis 27), thanks to the collaboration it requires between an artist or artists and a writer, the interanimations it showcases between word and image, and the intertextual possibilities it opens up with other visual and literary texts that it evokes through its visuals (from comics to canonical texts). Just as the picturebook is a "flexible form of text" (Lewis 44), the graphic novel, too, is a perpetually developing medium and it is the energy generated in this development that makes it such an exciting new medium, perfect for the university and college classroom.

NOTES

1. Much criticism has been devoted to the definition of this rich new medium. It is a term that is hotly contested. Even so, most critics identify Will Eisner's 1978 *A Contract with God and Other Tenement Stories* as the first graphic novel, though ironically it was not a novel at all but rather a collection of four interlinked stories. Alan Moore has dismissed the term as nothing more than a marketing device. In describing "the vital yet often misunderstood genre of the 'graphic novel'" (x), Charles Hatfield points to the sophistication and seriousness that the term "novel" accords to long-form comics. In turn, Stephen Tabachnick ironically points out that although graphic novels use the term "novel," many of them are actually nonfictional works, like autobiographies, biographies, histories, reportage, and travelogues. In their excellent analysis of the graphic novel, Jan Baetens and Hugo Frey clarify that the graphic novel has "a complex and variegated nature of form" (8), generally "tries to foreground more individual styles" (9), and tries to "turn away from [the] conventions" (9) of comics in its radical reformation of the comics genre as a whole. Recently the literary world's growing interest in comics and graphic novels legitimates both fields and absorbs them into the larger literary realm (Baetens and Frey 197), since, they note, "Literary adaptations have always been part of comics culture" (201). Baetens and Frey go on to argue that "a new space is being established by editors and publishers, where the frontiers between visual and literary culture are no longer present, and instead the two aspects conjoin to provide an attractive original offer to the public" (216). This exciting new medium undoubtedly "resists coherence" (xiii), as Charles Hatfield observes, and therein lies some of its power and possibility, both in and out of the university and college classroom.

2. This ideal that illustrated narratives will encourage readers (and students) to turn to literary texts is one that has been present in the marketing of comics from the beginning. Many early comics were published to draw young readers into the classics. The *Classics Illustrated* series, for example, was an important genre of comics, serving as a bridge to the English canon. Its tagline from 1950 onwards read: "Now that you have read the *Classics Illustrated* edition, don't miss the added enjoyment of reading the original, obtainable at your school or public library" (Baetens and Frey 39). Interestingly, issues of *Classics Illustrated* were released at the beginning of the new school year, and the Boy Scouts of America recommended their titles in their 1957 manual (ibid.). Comics thus aligned themselves early on with literature, both in an attempt to deepen literacy among youth and also to legitimize comics culture.

3. My insight into visual decoding is influenced by the work of E. H. Gombrich, Perry Nodelman, David Lewis, Maria Nikolajeva, and Carole Scott.

Works Cited

Allison, Marjorie C. "(Not) Lost in the Margins: Gender and Identity in Graphic Texts." *Mosaic,* vol. 47, no.4, 2014, pp. 73–97.

Baetens, Jan, and Hugo Frey. *The Graphic Novel: An Introduction.* Cambridge UP, 2015.

Barr, Robert B., and John Tagg. "From Teaching to Learning: A New Paradigm for Undergraduate Education." *Change,* vol. 27, no.6, 1995, pp. 12–26.

Carroll, Lewis. *Alice's Adventures in Wonderland and Through the Looking-Glass.* Oxford UP, 1998.

Carter, James Bucky. "Comics, the Canon, and the Classroom." *Teaching Visual Literacy,* edited by Nancy Frey and Douglas Fisher, Corwin Press, 2008, pp. 47–60.

Frey, Nancy, and Douglas Fisher. "Introduction." *Teaching Visual Literacy,* edited by Nancy Frey and Douglas Fisher, Corwin Press, 2008, pp. 1–4.

Hatfield, Charles. *Alternative Comics: An Emerging Literature.* UP of Mississippi, 2005.

Jenkins, Henry. *Convergence Culture, Where Old and New Media Collide.* New York UP, 2006.

Lewis, David. *Reading Contemporary Picturebooks: Picturing Text.* Routledge, 2001.

McCloud, Scott. *Understanding Comics: The Invisible Art.* HarperCollins, 1994.

McTaggart, Jacquelyn. "Graphic Novels: The Good, the Bad, and the Ugly." *Teaching Visual Literacy,* edited by Nancy Frey and Douglas Fisher, Corwin Press, 2008, pp. 27–46.

Michael, Joel. "Where is the evidence that active learning works?" *Advances in Physiology Education,* vol. 30, no. 4, 2006, pp. 159–67.

Miller, Frank and Lynn Varley. *300.* Dark Horse Books, 1999.

Moore, Alan, and Kevin O'Neill. *The League of Extraordinary Gentlemen,* Vol. 1. America's Best Comics, 2000.

Nodelman, Perry. *Words About Pictures: The Narrative Art of Children's Picture Books.* U of Georgia P, 1988.

Wolk, Douglas. *Reading Comics: How Graphic Novels Work.* Da Cap Press, 2007.

CHAPTER 7

"Does Doctor Manhattan Think?": Alan Moore's *The Watchmen* and a 'Great Books' Curriculum in the Early College Setting

Guy Andre Risko

When students first receive Alan Moore's *The Watchmen* in their second year (fourth semester) of the liberal arts seminar sequence at Bard High School Early College—Cleveland, an ease falls upon the shoulders of students throughout the room. After spending weeks with René Descartes' *Meditations on First Philosophy*, David Hume's *A Treatise on Human Nature,* and G. W. F. Hegel's *Philosophy of Mind,* the idea of reading a comic book feels like a lighter load. While the collection is physically much larger than something like the *Meditations,* student expectations control opening discussions about what they'll find within the story. During first reads, students glance over the pictures and focus almost exclusively on speech bubbles and plot. As deeper philosophical questions emerge about the nature of the detective novel or the counter-history hinted at by the subtext and visuality of the novel, students slowly wade into it with the intellectual seriousness that they easily grant to works they've been told are "important." While the sense of intellectual ease lessens over the course of the first week of discussion, it comes crashing down once the students realize the novel's central role in their two-year arc at Bard: the stakes of the philosophical questions we've debated are existential and global.

G.A. Risko (✉)
Bard High School Early College, Cleveland, OH, USA

© The Author(s) 2018
A. Burger (ed.), *Teaching Graphic Novels in the English Classroom,*
DOI 10.1007/978-3-319-63459-3_7

103

The emotional punch of this realization occurs at the end of the novel. At the top of page 375 of the *Watchmen* collection, the likely antagonist looks out at an audience made up of two figures and the reader. The speaker, dressed in purple and gold, talks directly, with force and clarity. Arguably the novel's most famous panel, it depicts not the temporal moment of narrative climax, but the climactic experience, the twist for the reader and their protagonist guides. In the panel, Antagonist Adrian "Ozymandious" Veidt says, "'Do it?' Dan, I'm not a Republic serial villain. Do you think I'd explain my *masterstroke* if there remained the slightest chance of you affecting its outcome? I did it thirty-five minutes ago" (Moore 375, emphasis original). Dan, the Nite Owl, and sociopathic detective Rorschach flank Veidt's figure, producing a panoptic visage. The decision to destroy all of New York in an attempt to unify global politics around a common enemy reflects the visual structure of the panel—all eyes are on Veidt, dressed as Ozymandious, the readers/listeners staring at a simulacra that unites everyone around him in confusion and horror. The two men stand in shock in the face of this ultimate moment of hyper-rationality, where Veidt's mode of thought subverts the genre conventions of the heroes. At the moment of reveal, reader and hero expectations are thrown away in the face of excessive reason/rationality. The characteristic violence that leads to peace in other comic books comes from the victory of the villain.

Within the narrative of *Watchmen*, Veidt's reveal and its resulting shock demonstrates the political and representational density of one of the most famous graphic novels within Western fiction. Its foundation comes from the generic expectations of both the hard-boiled detective novel and the 1950s superhero comic book, and exposes them to the conclusions of their own logical chains. The subversion of genre occurs along philosophical and political bounds, using the culture of the Cold War and the 1950s to confront the dangerous overzealousness of global nuclear annihilation made viable via Mutually Assured Destruction. In the case of both the superhero and detective novel genres *Watchmen* pulls from, the shared modes of thinking valorized crack and break under the weight of their own presuppositions about truth, rationality, and the ethical value of utilitarianism. In *Watchmen*, saving lives and finding the murderer do little to stop the death of millions. Departing from the genre conventions of the graphic novel, *Watchmen* produces a far-reaching, postmodern critique of rationalism made visible by Cold War political ideologies. However, far from simply critiquing the violent hyper-rationalism associated with the political ideologies of Mutually Assured Destruction, *Watchmen* confronts the intellectual premises and histories that undergird the faith in utilitarianism that such ideals relied upon. In the intervening years since the end of the Cold War and the changing global climate produced by the War on Terror, *Watchmen* has found ample room within the college classroom as a text that offers inroads to a history of political violence associated with American cultural dominance. This essay builds off the extant justifications of *Watchmen*'s inclusion in the college classroom to argue that its philosophical outlook on the nature of thought ought to allow it access to Great Books seminars. While the novel's critiques are narratively tied to the Cold War, in the contemporary classroom *Watchmen*'s intellectual value emerges from its deep pessimism about the potential for human thought to ward off the existential threats of our own making.

For students raised in the information age, long after the politics of surveillance and war became normalized in the wake of 9/11, *Watchmen* does not simply represent a response to postmodern war and the reckless disregard for humanity associated within the politics of "saving life."[1] By including a techno-god character in Dr. Manhattan, with knowledge of the position of every atom in the universe throughout time and space, this graphic novel moves beyond human politics toward the very metaphysical foundations of decision-making and action. *Watchmen* supports a theory of mind and decision-making that diverges heavily from traditional Enlightenment ideals found in works like René Descartes' *Meditations on First Philosophy*. This essay argues that *Watchmen* belongs in a seminar class not because of its traditionally lauded critique of Cold War politics, but because of its representation of the frailty of infinite, godlike knowledge. By building on the pedagogical framework that currently valorizes *Watchmen* as a particularly powerful text vis-à-vis political critique, the epistemologies associated with utilitarianism become even more tenuous and dangerous when abstracted away from any individual political moment. Dr. Manhattan's decisions to destroy Rorschach and leave Veidt to the political ecosystem his destruction has created produce a new theory of infinite knowledge as it occurs within temporally/earthly-bound experience. Dr. Manhattan's infinite power and knowledge become, in the wake of his own decisions to kill, fundamentally arbitrary. The narrative of *Watchmen* allows students to politically and philosophically question the veracity of knowledge as a way to improve decision-making.

The particular educational context this reading of *Watchmen* comes from is a complex and unique situation, which provides a series of challenges and goals that tests the plasticity and applicability of texts to a given theme. Bard

High School Early College—Cleveland is an extension of the liberal arts college in upstate New York and the location of my first deployment of this text within a Great Books seminar. Over the last two decades, Bard College began a series of extension programs aimed at folding those on the outside of elite liberal arts programs into its mission. At many of Bard's campuses, including early colleges, prisons, and international programs in locations like Palestine and St. Petersburg, students begin their college careers with a First Year Seminar.[2] During the fall and spring of their freshman year, Bard students take a seminar sequence that introduces them to the power of struggling with massive, complicated texts. Traditionally thought of as a "Great Books" course, the First Year Seminar attempts to acclimate students to the possibilities of thinking made possible by a liberal arts curriculum. These courses include a vast array of texts that stand as indispensable to the history of Western thought, including Virgil's *The Aeneid*, Dante's *Paradise Lost*, The Bible, and St. Augustine's *Confessions*. While texts and themes change occasionally, at any one time students are tasked with spending their collective first years interrogating crucial concepts and questions.

The Bard High School Early Colleges attempt to reach out to populations heretofore underserved by both the public school system in the United States and liberal arts schools historically designed to be a path toward social mobility. While each of the hybrid campuses (Manhattan, Queens, Harlem, Newark, Cleveland, and Baltimore) designs curriculum around their particular student needs and state requirements, each shares an extended version of Bard College's First Year Seminar that spans the four semesters of their college enrollment. At Bard High School Early College—Cleveland, students are placed in a dual-enrollment program where they simultaneously earn college and high-school credit. During the first two years, students complete the core requirements of most other high-school settings. In their third year, students transition to the college program. There, they have the opportunity to graduate with both their high-school diploma and an Associate's Degree after four years. By the end of their career, students experience the intense pressure of a broad and demanding education. In order to achieve such aims, the curriculum must both challenge and support students in a manner that pushes them to question their assumptions and affirm their agency and position within their world. Exposing them to texts like *Watchmen* aims to fulfill this goal.

At Bard's Early College in Cleveland, each of the four semesters of the students' third and fourth years asks students to consider a core question.

The semester discussed herein, the last of the four-semester sequence, is "What Is Thought?" Over the course of the semester, the class exposes students to texts that challenge their presumptions about what it means to think and comprehend ideas. At the core of the seminar sits the opening conversation between René Descartes' *Meditations on First Philosophy* and Moore's *Watchmen*. "What Is Thought?" aims to prove that the novel and the genre can stand on its own next to the traditionally considered "Great Works." The youth of the students, combined with the goals of the class, makes the educational situation within Bard High School Early College—Cleveland a fruitful and powerful place to test the veracity and greatness of *Watchmen* within a Great Books seminar.

Within extant literature on critical pedagogy, *Watchmen* takes up a position at the vanguard of graphic novels within the classroom. Few would argue against its inclusion in myriad literature classes: its artistic prowess, genre-confronting narrative, and deep ambivalence about the politics of its historical moment place it within a tier of literature valued for its postmodern predilections, regardless of (or despite) its formal considerations. The novel receives plaudits based on the clarity with which it enunciates the graphic novel as a tool in postmodern critique. The serialized nature of *Watchmen* allows for both issue-specific and series-long flashbacks and flash-forwards. For example, when Dr. Manhattan beams himself to Mars, the issue and the series oscillate between past and present while musing on the nature and potentiality of the future. In the first two panels of the first page of Chapter IV, Dr. Manhattan presents his knowledge of past, present, and future: "The photograph is in my hand ... They were in an amusement park, in 1959. In twelve seconds time, I drop the photograph to the sand at my feet, walking away. It's already lying there, twelve seconds into the future" (Moore 111). Dr. Manhattan can map time and space in all directions, granting him infinite knowledge of the whole of the cosmos. By the end of the novel, this knowledge, plus the ability to alter the atomic world, allows him to produce massive glass airships and life itself. In no uncertain terms, Dr. Manhattan illustrates the potential physical manifestations of infinite knowledge into the past and the future. However, this transcendental god, made out of the fruits of American ingenuity, only serves as a symbol of the frailty of human identity in the age of apocalypse. The sense of a frail, dangerous American identity has only grown since the 1980s, especially since the dawning of the current millennium.

In the wake of 9/11, the idea of American identity was once again tied tightly to existential threats to its existence. With this cataclysmic shift within public consciousness during the early 21st century, scholars began to speak highly of the role of *Watchmen* within the college classroom. These pedagogues pointed out the clear articulations of American ideology within the bounds of the global War on Terror. James Bucky Carter points out the vast contexts made available to students in grappling with the new sense of flux and insecurity produced by the attacks on 9/11:

> Our discussions of *Watchmen* within our contact zones and safe houses offered the most clarity we found in the aftermath of 9/11, because those in power around us were in the same situation: history was still being made, the connections still being sewn together as we came to terms with horrific images of buildings on fire and a new world of uncertainty. But the novel was too vast to cover in our short time and too complex for the class's level of literary experience. (107)

Carter's broad argument about the applicability of the text to post-9/11 memories ties itself to the particulars of historical social coherence—for Americans within the depths of the nuclear age and those confronted with the everyday potential of non-military attack, *Watchmen* spoke to the incoherence of their new fears and expectations. Carter's own experiences with the novel in the classroom speak to the various political and experiential avenues made available to readers of the text. As the "literary experience" Carter speaks about gets further and further from the lived reality of students within the college classroom, a philosophical framework may offer a provocative way of analyzing *Watchmen*.

The philosophical underpinnings of American culture serve as a primary source for philosophical readings of *Watchmen*. For example, Michael Prince connects the version of superheroes found in the novel to the American belief in the liberal individual as a crucial starting point for American identity. He argues that "while all of the characters in *Watchmen* exhibit some agency panic, most of them are possessed by a personally driven vigilantism that manifests autonomy and purposeful action attributed to the liberal individual" (Prince 817). Despite the attribution of the "superhero" moniker by a series of American citizens, their systems of belief all affirm the individualistic tendency that underwrites American ideology. Their individual ability to act emerges from their ability to read and predict the actions in the world. The inaction by the surviving heroes speaks to their ability to act, or not act, toward a perceived "greater good." Prince's articulation of liberal individualism evidences its problematic underbelly.

The desire to stay separate undergirds the moral ambiguity of the choices made by characters throughout *Watchmen* and the willingness of readers to accept value in the most ardent fascists without sensing any amount of ideological inconsistency.

These inclusions of *Watchmen* within the contemporary American studies classroom speak volumes to its propensity to evaluate Cold War culture with many of the most powerful tools postmodern narrative has to offer. *Watchmen* pieces together the core presuppositions of comic-book heroes and contorts their actions and outlooks via pastiche. A hero named "Rorschach" acts to test the readers' sense of moral absolutism in the face of violence and sexism, making the fourth wall a mirror into one's own psyche. The Nite Owl, a replacement for a retired and much-loved former cop, is doubly a copy: of the prior version of his moniker, and of the always in shape, hyper-masculine version found in the visage of Batman. The willingness of the United States to remove term limits because of the necessary stability of power in the face of total global victory at the hands of Dr. Manhattan's unexpected nuclear power magnifies the underlying logic of Mutually Assured Destruction and the neo-imperialism made manifest by the US's willingness to extend its nuclear power across the Western world. The novel's manipulation of genre expectations allows it to create a group of citizens with outsized personalities and totalized belief systems that still exist within a version of the Cold War fabric of US culture. This American, or Cold War-centric, focus, however, undersells the power of the novel itself. Even when abstracted beyond the historical and cultural circumstances intrinsic to its narrative, *Watchmen* offers students insight into some of the most long-debated questions within Western intellectual history. The novel's nuanced articulation of thought and being grants it a position alongside the works of René Descartes in explicating or articulating what it means to be a thinking thing.

Others have written about the philosophical underpinnings of this graphic novel, using characters as vehicles in understanding major debates within the field. James Digiovanna, in *Watchmen and Philosophy*, brings Dr. Manhattan into conversation with the nature of identity articulated by Descartes. Digiovanna gestures toward the impossibility of overcoming fundamental disagreements without being a real superhero. Following a clear line of thinking around the question "how am I the same person when I undergo so many changes," Digiovanna shows that Dr. Manhattan's ability to split himself into pieces and see through temporality allows him to actually achieve an answer to the question (104). Godlike power requires control over space and time, which Dr. Manhattan has in spades: "But Dr. Manhattan, by remembering both forward and backward in time, doesn't have this problem. This means that Dr. Manhattan has one super-power no one else has: he can overcome the philosophical problem of identity!" (Digiovanna 114). Dr. Manhattan's powers over the atomic world allow him to show the lengths of post-humanism necessary to crack the challenge of describing identity, a difficulty increased by changing understandings of science, technology, and the speculative power of the nuclear age. The political pressures of the Cold War produced the condi-tions for narrative curiosity associated with a new theory of the mind. In other words, political pressures associated with growing scientific power and progress produced a graphic novel that invented a necessary outlook on confronting hyper-rationality. In order to unearth this theory of mind, Dr. Manhattan must be put into a social context. His knowledge, on its own, presents an answer to the question of human identity; his actions, however, show that knowledge does not necessarily effect decision-making.

A close reading of *Watchmen* would be an appropriate place to start a defense of the inclusion of the novel within a Great Books seminar on the level of politics alone. In such a reading, I might point out the starting point of the novel, where the middle panel on page one foreshadows the whole of the narrative, a point of return so subtle and modernist in outlook that it gestures to the role rereading plays in coming to terms with the novel's difficulties. The page itself introduces readers to the crisp, clean lines and 3×3 panel layout that will stretch the length of the serial. The easy left-to-right, up-to-down visual layout appears natural and logical/organized, but is immediately shown to be insufficient for storytelling. The page slowly zooms out from ground level to the highest floor of a large apartment building. In doing so, each frame adds more and more context into the scene, telling the reader that limits on both space and time necessarily limit our own ability to think. Far from being a simple reiteration or retread of the philosophical debates over identity, experience, and representation, the pan up warns readers of the oppressive nature of narrative. The two speaking detectives who end the page cannot see the details of the case necessary for finding the "truth," that the killer is Ozymandious. In the middle of the opening page, this narrative arc, which visually represents the insufficiency of the eye and individual experience to find "truth," grants readers a single panel that represents the whole of the novel's arc. In walking through blood, overtop an unseen smiley face, Rorschach walks past the truck of the Veidt Company and his culprit. In the middle of the opening page, the major forces of the novel meet in a confluence that acts as collusion: Rorschach's insistence on his "moral" narrative forged in the gutter allows him to miss the truck; the monumental, all-seeing panoptic view of the police overlooks the system of streets that carry the "real" story of the Comedian's murder; and the readers have just been shown the identity of the killer through the unrecognized breaking of the fourth wall. Despite the crisp organization of the page, the clear drawings depicting the world through realism and grittiness, and the genre conventions associated with moral clarity, the presence of a counterweight to both the "police" and "vigilante" private eye undoes their individual projects. What we know, what we can know, and our own beliefs in epistemology are undone before the reader turns the first page. The novel, however, does not leverage just the postmodern distance associated with 1980s art and satire against the hegemony of hyper-rationality—it yearns to find a way to completely undo its viability as a political position.

Another avenue of close reading might follow the failure of (super) humans to control and usurp the nature of time and apocalypse. This philosophical reading points out the failure of human thought to separate moral decisions from individuality. A central trope of *Watchmen* writ upon both the narrative itself and in the symbolic economy of images within the novel emerges out of the Bulletin of Atomic Scientists' "Doomsday Clock." At the point of cataclysm at the climax of the novel, Adrian Veidt controls temporality in a seemingly totalized manner. He grants information to the reader only after his mission reaches fulfillment, pushing them thirty-five minutes into the past. When Veidt goes into a room full of televisions and sees dawning peace across the world, signified by the mobilization of military intelligence against an alien invasion, his victory pose is set to look like a clock a few minutes before midnight. Through the power of personality and planning, Veidt replaces the slow and unending march of time toward death with the power of human reason and deeply violent utilitarianism. At that moment of apparent victory, the final area of postmodern thought seems claimed by rationalism.

The two avenues of response to Veidt's apparent victory do not offer readers any real sense of hopefulness about the nature of human decision-making. On the one hand, Nite Owl and Silk Spectre, people who know that millions died at the hands of Adrian Veidt, have acclimated to living with a world of peace at any cost. Familial relations begin to heal and global capitalism seems to succeed with even greater ease. Two generations of Silk Spectre find avenues of reconciliation, and forgiveness between old antagonists occurs. Judging by the happiness of those with knowledge of the genocide, humans seem awfully willing to assent to total biopower if it leads to an increase in their own quality of life. At the end of the graphic novel, "progress," the linear improvement of humanity over time, is granted higher moral importance than the lives of millions of New Yorkers.

If the moral flexibility isn't harrowing enough, the other potential "end" to the novel may bring ethical optimism, but pessimism about the possibilities of human reason. In the face of a slower news cycle built in the engine of "peace," a person working in a fringe newspaper seems to find Rorschach's journal. Readers aren't privy to the real contents of it, nor the responses to it from this worker or the larger world. Yet, the foreboding sense of the scene points to a cyclical nature of human temporality, one where war and peace are two sides of the same, constantly flipping coin. Without Dr. Manhattan, finding out that an American business leader killed millions would throw the geopolitical situation back into the nuclear chaos that opens the novel. The limits on the human capacity for knowledge or actual utilitarian thinking are borne out at the experience of a great lie. Veidt's gamble requires the lack of information and the guarantee of the safety of all, not just the "most." Veidt's actions are fundamentally precarious, an impossible utopia that requires one hundred percent belief in personal safety. The novel's ambivalence over the nature of human thought and relationship to temporality, between the politics of progress and inevitability of cycles between war and peace, speaks a powerful message that goes beyond the pastiche nature of postmodernism: human thought and reason cannot be a starting point for the potential of morality.

In close readings like the ones described above, names like Martin Heidegger, Gilles Deleuze, Felix Guattari, William Spanos, Michel Foucault, Giorgio Agamben, and Judith Butler could be used to support the interesting representational choices of the novel. A more political reading might even talk about how the novel presages contemporary (non-)debates over the deaths of civilians in the global War on Terror, the rise of businessmen as political strongmen within Western democracies, and the ease of secrecy within the elite to keep the populace controlled. In each of these arcs, the novel might creep into the category of a "great" work, worthy of being read alongside philosophical and historical texts in humanities seminars. The real proof of this claim, however, is found in the novel's ability to produce a theory of the mind that critiques Enlightenment philosophy at its core. The particular strength of *Watchmen* comes from students' ability to formulate a theory of mind and thought that supports a merger of philosophy and politics, particularly by illustrating how political decisions offer counter-evidence for philosophical presupposition. Based on the experiences in the seminar class made up of young college students, centering the discussions on *Watchmen* allowed for a critique of Descartes through the production of an interpretation of "thought" found in the combination of content and form.

Within the space of the classroom, students quickly pointed out the role surprise plays in the novel's shift toward a stable, peaceful society at its conclusion, even with nuclear weapons. "He killed everyone!" said one student as we moved on to the second half of the text. The deep debate that followed our reading of Veidt's decision to destroy New York used the vocabulary from a previous semester on morality. Frameworks like "utilitarianism" were used to describe the decision; "moral absolutism" was placed on Rorschach as students analyzed the panel where he yells his final words to Nite Owl: "Never compromise" (Moore 402). Students debated about the justifications each character had for their moral outlook, wondering aloud if morals were a way of thinking or a way of acting. As the conversation continued, the subject shifted toward Dr. Manhattan's decision to kill Rorschach at the end, an addition that proved pivotal to the theorization about thought that followed from Descartes. The central political conceits of the novel, the battle between utilitarianism and deontology, between "I did it thirty-five minutes ago" and "never compromise," provide ample opportunities for students to engage in questions about moral decision-making. Dr. Manhattan allowed them to talk about the nature of thought, and how power and morality fundamentally affect that process.

Descartes' third meditation focuses on what knowledge can be built from the *cogito*. The argument for the existence of God that emerges from the third meditation sounds in many ways like Dr. Manhattan: "a substance infinite, independent, all-knowing, all-powerful ... the more attentively I consider them the less I feel persuaded that the idea of them owes its origin to myself alone" (Descartes 93). The finitude of human minds cannot produce a complete articulation of God. The experiential interactions characters have with Dr. Manhattan also follow this line of reasoning. Dr. Manhattan's immense power and ability to be everywhere at once means there is no singular point of experience that necessitates the fullness of his being. For example, Silk Spectre/Laurie Juspeczyk recoils at the idea of making love to many Dr. Manhattans at once and becomes even more upset at the fact that other incarnations of Dr. Manhattan continue to work on his science projects as they have sex. Here, Silk Spectre's reaction shows the proof of the Cartesian assessment; however, the immensity of Dr. Manhattan's power and increasing separation from human thought do not show that it can encompass his decision-making prowess. In other words, Descartes' argument that "he cannot be a deceiver, since . . . all fraud and deception spring from some defect" (97) is experientially untrue. Infinite access to information does not alter the nature of a decision-making framework. Deception, fraud, and other forms of morally problematic actions can still spring from omnipotence and omniscience. As one student put it, Dr. Manhattan's decision to eventually create life produces fear in the reader because the figure with the power to create sentience also allows for mass death for utilitarian reasons. That he will, eventually, create life does not mean his infinite knowledge produces moral righteousness. For students today, Dr. Manhattan's decision has very little to do with a political situation in particular and very much to do with the nature of human thought. *Watchmen* proves that omnipotence does not, in fact, separate gods from the frailty of the human imagination.

Beyond the fear of godly revenge sits a potential affirmation in human nature. In their reading of *Watchmen*, students recognized that the finitude of human experience is not a defect and, even if it could be seen as such, necessarily means that anything other than finitude is simply incomprehensible. The relationship between Dr. Manhattan and Silk Spectre easily draws the attention of students because of its doubly problematic nature: first because of the youth of Silk Spectre and second because of the apparently infinite knowledge Dr. Manhattan achieves through his very being. Despite this power dichotomy, by the end of the book students are unsurprised by the eventual coupling between Silk Spectre and Nite Owl. Both Silk Spectre and Dr. Manhattan are confused and off-put by their lover's reaction during their sexual moments, insinuating that even within the infinitude of omnipotence and omniscience, understanding remains difficult and outside the bounds of knowledge. In other words, the concept of the "good," or honesty, does not emerge naturally from the infinite mind of Dr. Manhattan, nor does it produce empathy. His access to the very neurons that fire in Silk Spectre's brain do not produce empathy, understanding, or, more importantly, knowledge of her desire. Knowledge of the mechanics of thought does not produce the knowledge one has of oneself. For *Watchmen*, not only does Descartes misunderstand the nature of God, he does so by undercutting self-realization.

Watchmen's theory of mind argues for the radical separation and independence of thoughts even within the world of an all-knowing, godlike figure. Dr. Manhattan's actions in killing Rorschach and leaving Veidt show that arbitrariness is ontologically consistent with human thought. Despite the knowledge that Dr. Manhattan could ensure the safety and security of the globe for eternity, at the end of the graphic novel, history remains indeterminate for readers. Veidt's utopia, the success of global commercialization, and the potential undoing of the project due to Rorschach's journal are left in a cloud of uncertainty. Despite our own limited knowledge of the future, shared with the humans within the novel, Dr. Manhattan shows no signs of not knowing what the future holds. For example, in Dr. Manhattan's last panel, he smirks at Veidt as he says "*Nothing* ends, Adrian. Nothing *ever* ends" (Moore 409, emphasis original). His decision to leave the Earth, then, speaks to his own indifference to human suffering. It also begs the question of his killing of Rorschach. Questions emerge about Dr. Manhattan's very nature, and whether or not his infinite capacity to think really makes him an arbiter of moral good. If his journal was to be found, why leave Rorschach dead? Simply because he asked? Why destroy life, if not to save more of it? If his journal is not going to be found, and killing Rorschach is a final act of helping humanity, then Veidt wins and the entire pastiche of superhero narratives rolls over in the face of violent utilitarianism and consumerism. The irreconcilable nature of Dr. Manhattan does not reduce to the goodness of Descartes' God; rather, it proves that infinite power still acts in the arbitrary manner of human frailty. In other words, the difference between God's knowledge and power and humanity's is one of scale, not quality.

In terms of a theory of mind and of thought, *Watchmen*'s answer to the role of God in how we know we are thinking beings is pessimistic and vague. The pastiche the graphic novel levies against Cold War politics produces a version of an all-powerful, godlike figure who either claims an interest in the killing as much as the saving of human lives, or wholeheartedly endorses the deaths of millions for the good of billions (and the survival of capitalism). While Cold War politics gained *Watchmen* entrance into the college classroom, its deep ambivalence about the meaning of infinite thought illustrates that it does not require that position in order to fit within academe. In fact, as existential crises change and students are faced with their own form of potentially infinite knowledge in the face of the internet, Dr. Manhattan offers a way of understanding the position global politics finds itself in with the persistence of nuclear weapons. In arguing against Descartes' *cogito*, *Watchmen* offers a theory of mind and thought that proves that, even with full knowledge, evil, genocide, and techno-capitalism remain fully possible. At the end of *Watchmen*, students see two roads diverging in a wood and in neither case does the accumulation of knowledge or the nature of thought lead toward moral or ethical perfection. The scariest aspect of *Watchmen* is that Dr. Manhattan's infinite knowledge and power still result in revenge-driven murder and the ascent to genocide. For students who have always lived in an age of nuclear weapons and a politics of global war, *Watchmen* offers an opportunity to see how limited perspectives manifest and allow for all manner of violent actions. Even in the face of immense power, actions do not, and cannot, be judged purely on outcome and results. Gods themselves act out of revenge, and should be viewed with deep skepticism.

Notes

1. See William V. Spanos, *America's Shadow* for an analysis of the destructive drive associated with maintaining the United States' version of capitalism globally via war-making: "It should not be overlooked that this … discourse repeats in *thought* the violence in *practice* to which the American officer in Vietnam synecdochically referred when he declared that '[w]e had to destroy Ben Tre in order to save it'" (204).
2. For more information about Bard College's First Year Seminar, see: www.bard.edu/fysem

Works Cited

Bernard, Mark, and James Bucky Carter. "Alan Moore and the Graphic Novel: Confronting the Fourth Dimension." *Interdisciplinary Comics Studies,* vol. 1, no. 2, 2004, http://www.english.ufl.edu/imagetext/archives/v1_2/carter/

Carter, James Bucky. "Teaching Watchmen in the Wake of 9/11." *Teaching the Graphic Novel,* edited by Stephen E. Tabachnick. Modern Language Association, 2009, pp. 99–108.

Descartes, René and Donald A Cress. *Meditations On First Philosophy.* Hackett 1993.

DiGiovanna, James. "Dr. Manhattan, I presume." *Watchmen and Philosophy: A Rorschach Test,* edited by Mark D. White, John Wiley & Sons, 2009: pp. 103–114.

Moore, Alan, and Dave Gibbons. *Watchmen.* Warner Books, 1987.

Prince, Michael J. "Alan Moore's America: The Liberal Individual and American Identities in Watchmen." *The Journal of Popular Culture,* vol. 44, no. 4, 2011, pp. 815–830.

Spanos, William V. *America's Shadow: An Anatomy of Empire.* U of Minnesota Press, 2000.

CHAPTER 8

"If He Be Mr. Hyde, We Shall Be Mr. See": Using Graphic Novels, Comic Books, and the Visual Narrative in the Gothic Literature Classroom

Allison Powell

One of the greatest challenges for the English teacher is finding a balance between educating students and entertaining them. This challenge continues to grow in the digital age, when students have hundreds of distractions at their fingertips. Teachers must compete with websites and apps that deliver information and entertainment through a variety of methods, even as the English classroom appears to be stuck in time, married to the idea of teaching classic texts in a traditional, text-centric manner. As the push toward data-driven educational methods increases, teachers must find a way to increase comprehension of the required curriculum. However, simply requiring students to read text, especially for more complex content such as the Gothic literature genre, is unlikely to improve scores, especially as data indicates reading comprehension ability is actually declining. The onus is on educators to find new and exciting delivery methods for complex texts. One simple yet still-underutilized approach is the introduction of more visual narratives into the text-centric content. Including the visual narrative genre in the Gothic literature classroom has the capacity to engage

A. Powell (✉)
Independent Scholar, Chandler, Arizona, USA

A. Burger (ed.), *Teaching Graphic Novels in the English Classroom*,
DOI 10.1007/978-3-319-63459-3_8

the reluctant reader, support the struggling reader, and offer a greater likelihood of overall comprehension of Gothic literature's complex themes.

Julia Round states that Gothic literature is "a response to social trauma—a subversive and critical way of addressing problems in society" (55). Because of this, Gothic can "subsume genre ... and cross media" (ibid.). She argues that there is no one "Gothic" genre, which explains why Gothic elements can be found in the works of Stephen King and in the storylines of *Scooby Doo*; it can absorb other genres, which means westerns and science-fiction pieces can—and do—have Gothic elements. It also means comics can apply Gothic themes, which Round notes those published near the end of the 20th century did especially effectively, in light of Y2K and other apocalyptic fears. Additionally, because much of the Gothic text is often symbolic in nature—walking down a staircase can signify descent into madness; literal and metaphorical darkness blend into one; a decaying manor house conveys the decay of society—its constructs are ripe for the picking by the visual narrative.

Up until recent decades, however, the graphic novel genre was considered by literary scholars to be a less than respectable form of narrative. Comics were widely panned in favor of text-only writing, and those who read comics for pleasure were considered by the literary elite to be the dregs of the reading public. That stigma continues for some today, as demonstrated by Christine Ferguson's university students' reluctance to embrace graphic novels along with the traditional canon of university literature. Though these same students may not object to graphic novels per se, Ferguson has observed that they struggle to accept them as intellectually appropriate pieces "on a university syllabus." Others fail to see how exaggerated comic depictions of 19th-century England can accurately represent the culture of the time. In recent years, though, the graphic genre has experienced a renaissance of popularity and consideration. George Dardess reminds readers that text and graphics have been combined for millennia, from the pictographs found on the walls of Egyptian tombs to "Bayeux tapestry ... and in the blending of words and pictorial art by William Blake," and asserts that the graphic genre has always been "a form appealing to the masses." Ferguson also notes the popularity of illustrated serials during the Victorian era. Comics especially were born out of the invention of mass media in the form of periodicals and newspapers. Like other forms that appeal to the masses—the lower classes—then, comics have "been met with indifference and even at times with fear and hostility from higher, more educated groups" (Dardess), and it wasn't until the mid 1990s that the "centuries-old barrier . . . show[ed] signs of crumbling" (ibid.). One major sign that this barrier continues to crumble is academic study on comics and graphic novels, most notably in the works of Scott McCloud, whom Dardess refers to as "the savior." McCloud's book *Understanding Comics* has almost single-handedly given an authority to comics and the visual narrative by proving they can be considered as more than simple picture stories. Certainly McCloud's book has not broken down all resistance to visual narrative, even more than two decades after its publication, but it allows and even invites the skeptic to really examine how the visual narrative has not been proven detrimental to readers, and opens up the possibility of using a more graphic format to teach traditional texts.

THE GRAPHIC SHAKESPEARE

When it comes to traditional texts, it is hard to find ones more traditional than the plays of William Shakespeare, and there have been multiple attempts to apply a graphic approach to the Bard. Shari Sabeti describes two different graphic novel versions of *Hamlet* that have been written and used in schools already. One of these uses the original wording along with futuristic Manga, while the other creates a contemporary translation of sorts, but remains fairly true to the Elizabethan imagery. The creators of *Self Made Hero*, the Manga version of *Hamlet*, assert that because this form of graphic novel is a genre popular with both genders, it is likely to not only meet curriculum requirements but also appeal to younger readers, engaging them with Shakespeare more than they may have been before, due to the assumption that "Shakespeare is opaque and it is not easy to become literate in it without some mediating aid" (Sabeti 186). Sabeti compares this version to the 1996 Baz Luhrmann film version of *Romeo + Juliet*: original wording in a contemporary setting. Conversely, SparkNotes, the company behind the contemporary-language version, offers students the opportunity to be closer to the original setting of the play rather than the original language, differentiating themselves from *Self Made Hero* by "placing an emphasis on [Shakespeare's] 'word'" (Sabeti 189) rather than his words. Ultimately, Sabeti asserts that both of these comic versions of *Hamlet* will be key in helping educators determine best practices for "the way in which literacy is constructed through adapted texts and how different kinds of 'profit' . . . circulate through such processes" (196).

Though Sabeti concludes that there is still research to be done on the use of different delivery methods of Shakespeare, Amy Maynard asserts more directly that there is a benefit to using comics in order to help students learn Shakespeare. She not only notes how interest in reading Shakespeare constantly ranks almost last in polls of British teenage students, but also that interest in reading is generally low (Maynard 96). Addressing, indirectly, Sabeti's concern about the different ways in which groups will profit from different delivery methods of Shakespeare, Maynard explains that while "there are certain expectations when studying Shakespeare" (100), new ways of interpreting the Bard have become prevalent and parallel to the course of analysis of popular culture. As such, "when analysing Shakespeare in a pop cultural context, it can help to ease the added burdens of having to address the inevitable differences that exist between a reader in the 21st century and a man creating works that date back to the Elizabethan age" (ibid.). Simply put, Maynard accepts that understanding Shakespeare means allowing the adaptation of the presentation of Shakespeare, and comic books are an appropriate way to ensure delivery of curricular standards within an engaging and culturally appropriate medium. This is an important point, as many educators may tend to forget that the plays read in classrooms across the world were meant to be performed, not simply read, and experienced in a contemporary manner that today is considered Elizabethan theatre. To merely read one of Shakespeare's plays within the confines of a book, then, does nothing to help the student comprehend the text in the medium in which it was originally intended or delivered. In the end, Maynard's assertion has nothing to do with reading scores or ensuring that the traditional learning of Shakespeare continues in the classroom, but rather that "most importantly, children are starting to take an interest in Shakespeare, ensuring that his legacy will live on" (108). This may be key in all areas of literature: it isn't just a matter of ensuring that a student can achieve high marks on a test, but that he reads the material in the first place.

Textual Literacy and Engagement

It is, then, largely a matter of shaking up the delivery of the literary canon without necessarily shaking up the canon itself. This approach isn't necessarily new, nor is it reserved only for the method of delivering the text itself. John V. Knapp asserts, "Most of us enjoy a change now and then, whether to a different brand of ice cream or to a method by which we teach the 'classic' works of literature." His reasoning is based on Yashikazu Kobayashi's assertion that "presenting information [lecturing] guaranteed to be correct by authorities is not sufficient for the construction of knowledge" (qtd. in Knapp). That is, traditional lecture, even if it conveys accurate information, is not going to be enough to ensure students will gain knowledge of a topic. If they cannot gain knowledge, the lowest level of learning of Bloom's Taxonomy, it is highly unlikely they will be able to synthesize the information. For his own classes, Knapp created a game to help students understand George Orwell's *Animal Farm* that departed from the traditional lecture and drill method of discussion, in which the instructor asked questions that would guide students to the correct answers. Knapp's game, Animal Farm Hegemony, was a "deliberate echo of the board game, *Monopoly*" but with an emphasis on gaining power as well as wealth. The game sought to enhance student comprehension of the socialist allegory of the novel by gaining understanding of their own "ethical values and procedures." Though the game, which was bookended by more traditional lecture methods during the unit, was created nearly two decades ago and may be dated because of the technological limitations of the mid-1990s when contrasted with today's classroom, it demonstrates the desire teachers consistently have to find unconventional and exciting ways to help the literature reach students.

The idea of reaching more students will likely lead educators to exploring comics as a means to help struggling and/or unengaged readers with more complex material like Gothic literature, especially as reading ability levels have declined by approximately three grade levels in the last century (Krusemark 47), a trend that does not appear to be reversing. Maynard discusses a study of librarians that "confirmed the hypothesis that graphic novels inspire reluctant readers to participate in recreational reading" (Maynard 104). Since "horror and comics have a long and intertwined history" (Round 7), purposeful inclusion of the visual narrative is likely to coax lower- and non-readers into the material, allowing them to make meaning in a more multimodal facilitation. David E. Low suggests that the panels in comic books can help struggling readers decode and learn the literal text (372–373), making it ideal for use in a Gothic literature unit, as Gothic texts assume that basic reading comprehension skills have long since been mastered when, many times, they have not.

But while there is temptation to focus on using what appear to be simple texts to help bridge the gap for underperforming readers, graphic novels show promise for all students. Both Ferguson and Renee Krusemark discuss how college students read comics for pleasure and how that has led to their use in the undergraduate classroom. Low asserts that comics are not simple texts but rather "complex works of literature in their own right that can enable students to develop into critical readers" (Low 375). Krusemark further remarks that comic books contain "rare words" an average of 53 times per 1,000 words; in comparison, an adult-level novel contains an average of 52 "rare words" per 1,000 words. The complexity of comics, then, is on a par with grade-level-appropriate texts at the secondary level (Krusemark 47). Krusemark speculates that comics, because of their inherent approachability, can provide all students an opportunity to tackle not only complex texts but complex subjects, such as the themes and conventions found in Gothic literature. Seeing the two extremes in weather in Mary Shelley's *Frankenstein; or, The Modern Prometheus*, for example, can allow students to comprehend this motif and make informed predictions about the action in the plot when they come upon the next weather change.

Like Low, Janette Hughes and Alyson E. King decry comics being promoted solely as simpler options for struggling readers and argue that they can require "even more complex reading skills than traditional print texts," skills which are vital today as different forms of media, such as Facebook, Twitter, and YouTube, have "expanded the ways in which texts are read and received, as well as ways in which communication occurs." One aspect that can stand out for those seeking to teach Gothic literature pieces such as Robert Louis Stevenson's *Strange Case of Dr. Jekyll and Mr. Hyde*[1] via graphic medium is how comics can convey moments of silence in a way that words simply cannot. Ian Campbell points out that it is difficult to put onto film what is mostly an internal struggle (56). Jekyll's "perennial war among [his] members" (Stevenson 48), which ultimately brings about the manifestation of Hyde, isn't a scene that can be easily acted out and projected onto the big screen. However, this internal struggle and outward silence can be shown graphically, whether conveyed as hesitation via ellipses and other semiotic devices within a speech bubble, or even through the lack of speech bubbles for multiple panels, as noted when Hughes and King examine Michel Rabagliati's *Paul Has a Summer Job*. Of course, the space in each panel is limited, whereas a paragraph or book has only the limitations of the author's word choice. Because of these limits, graphic novels allow the authors to use a "show don't tell" approach that requires deeper examination and analysis by the reader, which is one of the multiliteracies examined by Hughes and King via Jillian Tamaki and Mariko Tamaki's comic *Skim*. Overall, Hughes and King assert that "graphic novels offer new ways to engage with texts and can be exciting vehicles for critically exploring relevant issues with students of all abilities." Since students of any ability level can partake in comics reading as appropriate to their learning level, comics become an ideal option for the ever-growing population of special-needs students who are integrated into the mainstream classroom. Comics, then, may differentiate learning more easily and more confidentially than different complexity levels of the same novel might. But since the "Gothic [genre] also holds the active reader at its center" (Round 56), including the Gothic comic just might make the entire class more engaged, too.

Visual Literacy and Critical Thinking

Comics can certainly provide teachers a means of facilitating textual literacy in the classroom, but they also serve as a valuable tool in establishing visual literacy. Andrew F. Schroeder reminds us that literature has a history of using visual cues, from the *New England Primer* to a woodcut pictorial version of Lewis Carroll's *Alice in Wonderland/Through the Looking Glass.* This brings to light the merit of teaching comics as a viable genre via a semiotic approach; that is, comics, in their use of a combination of images and text—both valid means of communication for millennia—offer many opportunities by which students can make meaning of a piece in ways that are unique to the graphic genre. Additionally, Schroeder argues that "The use of images and language to communicate meaning is a deceivingly complex process, and a critically important one" (28). Traditional texts at the high-school level do not offer many—if any—images from which the reader can negotiate different meanings. The combination of the two "requires active participation from the reader in order to continuously fill in the gutters between panels" (33). Since comics are a series of pictures with some text, the reader is charged with filling in the blanks, as it were, in order to have the full comprehension that a traditional text would outline with more words. Because of this complexity, reading comics appeals to a broad variety of readers, from those who struggle to those who are stronger, yet just not engaged for a variety of reasons. Further, "Teaching with comics provides opportunities to address a variety of visual literacy skills required by the common core" (Schroeder 127). Ultimately, Schroeder concludes that the teaching of comics "should be acknowledged as valuable material worth incorporating into literacy classes" (127–128). Certainly, then, if comics can help students become engaged in challenging content such as Shakespeare, they can be considered for mastery of Gothic devices and texts.

As a result of their textual and visual complexity, both comics and Gothic literature require critical-thinking skills. Low's attention to the gutters, the space between the images in comics, underscores how students must use critical thinking skills in order to read "between the lines" (382). This practice helps students learn to make inferences: "If Spider-Man is swinging above the streets of New York City in one panel and then riding atop a speeding car in the next, how did he get there?" (Low 378). Such inferences are necessary in Gothic literature, in which externality is rarely present. The question about Spider-Man above can be applied analogously to understanding Jekyll's motives for financially providing for Hyde long before the final chapter, in which all is revealed. In fact, using gutters carefully in a graphic representation of *Strange Case of Dr. Jekyll and Mr. Hyde* may possibly make up for what cannot be externalized within the panels. Similarly, Krusemark found that readers of *The Walking Dead*, a comic series with several Gothic elements, were able to identify various leadership skills displayed by characters in the series and by that infer what it took to make a real-life leader. She theorizes that using comics such as *The Walking Dead* "may help improve deficient critical thinking skills in college students while also exploring new methods of teaching critical thinking that some researchers consider to be insufficient" (Krusemark 132). As such, comics appear to be a promising source for developing critical-thinking skills.

These critical-thinking skills are increasingly necessary in today's society, in which people can engage with the technology available to them, often without fear or even thought of repercussion. Jené M. Fletcher discusses how the means of technology allowed Henry Jekyll access to certain freedoms he otherwise would not have had. This, Fletcher argues, is an essential theme of Stevenson's novella: the ease with which technological advances make certain life choices more accessible and thus more tempting, despite their possible consequences. He points out that Jekyll's actions—both the creation of the tincture that turns him into Hyde and the activities in which he is able to partake as his alter ego—are done in secret, mostly behind closed doors. Though he is visible as Hyde in public, the transformation itself is never seen by anyone until the incident with Dr. Lanyon, at which point Jekyll is already dying and desperate for help. Yet this occasion was still only visible to the chosen audience: Lanyon. The question as to whether or not what one does behind closed doors can or should be judged is central to Fletcher's examination of the novella. Though he doesn't focus at all on the modern comic genre, Fletcher's questioning of the ethical use of technology is certainly as applicable today as it was when technology meant the acquiring of specific salts with which to make a solution. However, when compared with Marvel Comics' story of Dr. Bruce Banner/The Hulk, the reader is confronted with the fact that scientists continue to push boundaries that should perhaps not be pushed. As technology dependence grows in the 21st century, individuals are presented with this same dilemma, but without the benefit of seeing consequences to their actions, as they may be able to do within the pages of Stevenson's work. Offering the comparison of Jekyll to Banner and then applying it to contemporary social contexts allows the reader to take a larger look at the possible consequences of knowledge for the sake of knowledge and the race to the top of an imagined mountain. As such, Fletcher's study can lend itself to the argument that, regardless of the time period, *Strange Case of Dr. Jekyll and Mr. Hyde* is relevant. Teaching the novella and its Gothic kin can allow students to examine their own decision-making by means of critical-thinking techniques; in a sense, a sort of individual soul-seeking and coming to terms with one's decisions, even when that results in the uncomfortable realization of improper technological application.

Drawbacks

Of course, presenting visual narrative in a Gothic literature course becomes problematic when attempting to put into pictures that which Gothic authors left off the page. Campbell reminds us that several film iterations of Gothic classics such as *Strange Case of Dr. Jekyll and Mr. Hyde* and *Frankenstein* have done poorly because it is nearly impossible for a viewing audience to go through the plot with the same uncertainty and lack of external detail with which a reader goes through these same books. He points out that the majority of the book is based upon speculation by the reader; nothing is revealed until the end. As such, film versions disallow for the "shying-away from the facts" (Campbell 52) because the audience needs something to see; attention is diverted away from the account Victor Frankenstein gives to Robert Walton and onto the laboratory in which Victor conducted his strange experiment. Even at the end of *Strange Case of Dr. Jekyll and Mr. Hyde*, when the details about Jekyll's experiment are revealed, Campbell notes that the specific information is still unknown. The actual ingredients, aside from a salt, remain a mystery, and Jekyll's physical transformation isn't externalized: "It is the *internalised* vision of change, not the scientific or quasi-scientific transformation which so shocks Lanyon, but which we never once see properly in the narrative" (Campbell 57, emphasis original). It would be impossible for a graphic novel to show the internal change Henry Jekyll undergoes to become Edward Hyde; physical change cannot fully convey the transformation from essentially good to absolute evil. Even the best artists cannot convey that. But even the physical characteristics alone would be difficult for an artist to convey. The horror that builds up in Utterson's narrative in *Strange Case of Dr. Jekyll and Mr. Hyde* doesn't play well on screen because a visual audience would demand to see Hyde, even though Hyde's indescribability is repeated several times throughout the novella, from Enfield's first explanation of the incident he witnessed and his reflection that "He is not easy to describe" (Stevenson 11), to the inability of those witnesses Utterson interviews to describe Hyde with any amount of tangibility, as "the few who could describe him differed wildly; and that was the haunting sense of unexpressed deformity with which the fugitive impressed his beholders" (Stevenson 24). The only way in which Hyde is reliably described is as giving the impression of having some sort of physical deformity, even though he doesn't outwardly display one. Presenting a student with a graphic form of this novella, then, problematizes Hyde in that he must become describable. Further, the artist's rendering needs to be able to show Hyde for what he is without giving away he is the alter ego to Henry Jekyll.

Gordon Hirsch reminds the reader that in both *Strange Case of Dr. Jekyll and Mr. Hyde* and *Frankenstein*, the hideousness of Hyde and the creature, respectively, are conveyed, but it is still "the *impression* [of the character] that counts rather than any particularized physical description" (225, emphasis original). He goes on to argue that "the appearance of the double [either Hyde or the creature] is not to be concretely visualized, but its effects on those who behold it are deeply felt" (Hirsch 226). Because both Hyde and the creature were born of desire, an intangible itself, they cannot be described with mere words, because those words automatically set parameters for appearance. If Hyde were described as having green eyes, or brown hair, the graphic representation would be able to convey that precisely. But neither Hyde nor the creature are given observable modifiers, and it is up to the reader to imagine what Hyde's "displeasing" (Stevenson 11) appearance really looks like. Even as the reader sees in the development of Edward Hyde, the character cannot conform to any set of visual standards. He changes throughout the novella, and as his looks can never be put into words, Utterson is only able to define that he has grown in stature from the beginning of the book to the end. Of course, in putting *Strange Case of Dr. Jekyll and Mr. Hyde* into the visual narrative, the very rendering of Hyde becomes troublesome. If he doesn't look the same each time Utterson comes across him—or when anyone comes across him, as if he were some sort of boggart walking among us—it is difficult to imagine how he would appear in subsequent panels, even on the same page. The question as to whether the reader would recognize him as Hyde each time must be raised, as does the concern that while an image of Hyde certainly may be what the artist imagines, if Hyde does indeed evolve as the evil within him grows, it is impossible to say how a reader may imagine him. Creating a graphic representation of a character who defies description and seemingly changes his appearance presents a unique challenge, then, and reminds the Gothic literature teacher that if a visual narrative is to be used, it must still be able to convey the uncertainty that the author(s) embedded into the text. It is less necessary for a character like Hyde to have a specific look than it is for the reader to develop the same sense of dread and horror as originally intended.

Gothic and the Modern Comic

While, certainly, the Gothic literature teacher needs to be aware of possible limitations to the visual narrative, these do not outweigh the possible benefits to students in terms of learning themes of the genre. The very universality of Gothic literature's social commentary is woven into the pages of popular comic books today, which allows for this less traditional take on the canon of Gothic writings as well. Marvel's Stan Lee, arguably the best-known comic creator to date, stated that he decided his characters needed to "be the kind of characters I could personally relate to ... they'd have their faults and foibles, they'd be fallible and feisty, and—most important of all— ... they'd still have feet of clay" (qtd. in Cassidy 55). This is what the reader sees in two key Marvel characters in particular: Ben Grimm/The Thing and Bruce Banner/ The Hulk. Both of these characters have almost obvious similarities with Henry Jekyll and Edward Hyde; they are the same two beings within one body, they are nearly polar opposites of each other in terms of morality— though Craig Cassidy points out that Jekyll was not an absolute angel to Hyde's absolute devil—and they do not see an improvement in their life after being split into two personas. Cassidy even explains that, in having these two sides, while in some ways a benefit to society as a whole, the bestowal of superpowers becomes "a blessing and a curse" (63), which the reader can infer when reading Henry Jekyll's account of the affair in the final chapter of

Stevenson's work. Robin J. Dugall acknowledges the degree to which internalized anxiety, such as Jekyll's desperation to remain a part of polite society, or Banner's desire to use science to make the world more perfect, despite the flaws in his masculinity, is made more difficult to bear than one shared by society, because "Facing the truth about ourselves hurts like hell" (145). The imperfections of both Banner and the attack-ready Hulk are much easier to acknowledge when pointing the finger at someone else. But as difficult as this is, Dugall asserts that looking at ourselves in terms of the green comic-book antihero allows us to better ask those "deeper questions related to our own psyche" (145) as we "battle with the depth of human existence" (146). Dugall, like Thomas Donaldson and Stan Lee himself, acknowledges that the Hulk is an example of an imperfect character but one readers can have empathy for and with, which makes him more identifiable. Thus, the battle to control the Banner/Hulk body, Dugall argues, is symbolic of the internal struggle taking place inside each person as to whether or not to descend into brawn instead of brain; for, as Donaldson maintains, as the Hulk has evolved, his similarities with Banner's intelligence level have ebbed away; contemporary iterations present him speaking in Neanderthal-like grunts instead of complete, articulate sentences. Literature, regardless of the genre, is about connecting with the reader, and if a reader can connect with the internal battle of Banner/Hulk, Occam's razor suggests that he has the ability to connect to that same battle between Jekyll and Hyde or Victor Frankenstein and his creation.

That ability of the reader to identify with flawed characters such as Ben Grimm/The Thing and Bruce Banner/The Hulk makes these characters ideal for showing students how much both Gothic literature and visual narrative are calls for a change in social norms and how society evolves from one era and set of concerns to another. Cassidy notes that comic-book characters, like Peter Parker/Spider-Man, "grew and evolved simultaneously with [their] readers" (78). Stevenson was known to have never truly explained what he wanted readers to take from *Strange Case of Dr. Jekyll and Mr. Hyde*, so it is up to the reader, and the culture in which that reader grew up, to make meaning of the book and its ambiguities. The very evolution that makes Peter Parker/Spider-Man, Ben Grimm/The Thing, and Bruce Banner/The Hulk all fit into the cultural expectations and needs of a given time period is the same evolution that allows Stevenson's work to remain relevant and even contemporary. For example, *The Incredible Hulk*, when it was originally published, conveyed "a crisis of masculinity" (Donaldson 441) that was prevalent during the atomic age of the post-World War II decades. Bruce Banner and the Hulk are competing male roles; Banner is the weak intellectual while the Hulk is raw testosterone. Put more succinctly: "Banner is *hypo*masculine, the Hulk is an image of hypermasculinity" (Donaldson 436, emphasis original). The modern-day *Avengers* film series, though, focuses less on the struggle to find oneself somewhere between the two extremes of the original Banner and Hulk and more on the internal struggle of those with mental illness and how emotions can take control of a person and wreak havoc, emphasized most clearly when Dr. Banner tells Captain America "I'm always angry" before transforming effortlessly into the Hulk. Likewise, a contemporary understanding of *Strange Case of Dr. Jekyll and Mr. Hyde* may result in the examination of drug use and overdose to combat internal struggle instead of the contemplation of the consequences caused by the repression of desires, as it may have when the novella was first published.

The ability of the comic-book protagonist, whether the perfect hero or the Byronic one, to evolve with his reader, also allows the reader to identify Gothic themes and devices in different settings. The evolution of DC's Bruce Wayne/Batman displays the continued relevance of the commentary of the Gothic genre by what Alex Wainer calls his "mythic ... nature" (15). Drawing differences between myths and the mythic, Wainer explains that while mythic stories may use myths, which he determines as those ancient creation stories, the mythic focuses more on the "figures, motifs, narrative patterns, and symbols which have their origin in myths proper" (21), but they are not myths in themselves. He gives the example of the western-genre movie: the myth of the Wild West began in the early 1930s, but by the time television programs like *Gunsmoke* and *Bonanza* came along a few decades later, audiences were used to the formula of the western, at which point the genuine westerns began being replaced with parodies, the best known being Mel Brooks's *Blazing Saddles*, which adhered to the same formula and conventions of earlier films starring John Wayne but put a satirical spin on the plot for comedic value.

The creators of *Batman*, then, took aspects from "our cultural legacy" (Wainer 26) to produce a character who is seemingly new with every iteration but yet, in terms of bat folklore, centuries old. Over the decades, Batman has progressed in a fashion similar to the western, although he has also been able to cycle back from the last, parodic phase of the 1960s television series to something new and even "primitive" (Wainer 53). While the character remains largely the same, various adaptations of the comic's "presentational style" (ibid.), along with updates to his gadgets, physical abilities, and technology, provide for Bruce Wayne/Batman to have a life cycle similar to that of the immortal jellyfish. What makes Bruce Wayne/Batman continuously compelling, regardless of his iterations, is the romantic archetype his character takes on: someone who has lost something via great tragedy and who turns that "loss into a crusade, which becomes the core of his mythic appeal" (Wainer 71). He is both romantic in the fictionalized, unrealistic sense and in the persona of a Romantic hero, one who is flawed yet acts upon his Sturm und Drang-esque emotions in order to improve his Gotham City society. Even Batman's preference for vigilante justice over cooperation with law enforcement evokes the British Romantics' suspicion of the establishment. With the close ties between the Romantic and Gothic movements, this is where parallels to Gothic literature in the classroom must not be ignored; much of Gothic literature is British or American, and if a reader is going to recognize the mythic archetypes that make the Batman series continually successful, they will largely be able to recognize those same ideas in the traditional Gothic text, so long as the ability to make the jump is offered.

CONCLUSION

The adaptability of Gothic literature makes it the ideal genre for comic book education. Parallels between Henry Jekyll/Edward Hyde and Bruce Banner/The Hulk or Ben Grimm/The Thing are impossible to ignore, as are the parallels with the commentary both comics and Gothic literature make about society's ills. Gothic literature is nothing if not subversive, and a social commentary by means of intellectual terror and horror, and in many ways, contemporary comic books do the exact same thing. Ultimately, including visual narratives in the Gothic literature curriculum will continue to do the most important job, and the one that keeps students reading: giving them an opportunity to engage with the text. Graphic novels and comics are far from simplistic, watered-down versions of classics that can begin to bridge the gap with lower readers; they are rich, complex texts that can engage readers of all levels and offer them the opportunity to delve deeper into a text for greater comprehension. Gothic literature continues to be relevant today, offering readers a way to understand the darker elements of the human psyche. As the world continues to change and evolve into a digital-centric one that holds the visual up as a key element in comprehension, presenting literature in ways that include visual representation will be key to keeping the classics alive and valid. Gothic literature has proven it can be contemporary in each time period. Including the visual narrative when presenting Gothic literature will guarantee that it continues to be for years to come.

NOTE

1. Often referred to and republished as *The Strange Case of Dr. Jekyll and Mr. Hyde*, Stevenson did not use "The" in his original title, a choice that is replicated by the Norton Critical Edition of this text, which "is based on the 1886 First British Edition, [and] the only edition set directly from Stevenson's manuscript and for which he read proofs." In keeping with this formatting, I have included the original version of the title, *Strange Case of Dr. Jekyll and Mr. Hyde*.

WORKS CITED

The Avengers. Directed by Joss Whedon, performances by Mark Ruffalo and Chris Evans, Marvel Studios, 2012.

Campbell, Ian. "Jekyll, Hyde, Frankenstein and the Uncertain Self." *Cahiers Victoriens et Edouardiens: Revue du Centre d'Etudes et de Recherches Victoriennes et Edouardiennes de l'Université Paul Valéry, Montpellier,* vol. 40, 1994, pp. 51–62.

Cassidy, Craig. *Marvels, Heroes, and Gods: A Depth Psychological Journey into the Marvel Comics Universe of the 1960s.* 2012. Pacifica Graduate Institute, PhD Dissertation.

Dardess, George. "Bringing Comic Books to Class." *Contemporary Literacy Criticism,* edited by Janet Witalec, vol. 1777, 2004. Originally published in *College English,* vol. 57, no. 2, Feb. 1995, pp. 213–222.

Donaldson, Thomas. "The Strange Case of Doctor Banner and the Incredible Hulk: Masculine Anxiety in the Atomic Age as Shown in the Pages of Marvel Comics' The Incredible Hulk." *The Image of the Outsider II,* edited by Will Wright and Steven Kaplan. Society for the Interdisciplinary Study of Social Imagery, University of Colorado-Pueblo, 2008, pp. 434–442.

Dugall, Robin J. "Running from or Embracing the Truth Inside You? Bruce Banner and the Hulk as a Paradigm for the Inner Self." *The Gospel According to Superheroes: Religion and Pop Culture,* edited by B.J. Oropeza, Peter Lang Publishers, 2005, pp. 145–154.

Ferguson, Christine. "Steam Punk and the Visualization of the Victorian: Teaching Alan Moore's *The League of Extraordinary Gentlemen* and *From Hell.*" *Teaching the Graphic Novel,* edited by Stephen E. Tabachnick, The Modern Language Association, 2009, pp. 200–207.

Fletcher, Jené M. "Technology Gone Wrong: The Science and Ethics of Dr. Jekyll and Mr. Hyde." *Nineteenth-Century Literature Criticism*, edited by. Lawrence J. Trudeau, vol. 292. Originally published in *The Image of Technology*, edited by Will Wright and Steven Kaplan, Society for the Interdisciplinary Study of Social Imagery, University of Colorado-Pueblo, 2009, pp. 111–113.

Hirsch, Gordon. "*Frankenstein*, Detective Fiction, and *Jekyll and Hyde*." *Dr. Jekyll and Mr. Hyde After One Hundred Years*, edited by William Veeder and Gordon Hirsch, University of Chicago Press, 1988, pp. 223–246.

Hughes, Janette, and Alyson E. King. "Dual Pathways to Expression and Understanding: Canadian Coming-of-Age Graphic Novels." *Children's Literature in Education,* vol. 41, no. 1, Mar. 2010, pp. 64–84.

Knapp, John V. "Creative Reasoning in the Interactive Classroom: Experiential Exercises for Teaching George Orwell's *Animal Farm.*" *Short Story Criticism*, edited by Joseph Palmisano, vol. 68. Originally published in *College Literature*, vol. 23, no. 2, June 1996.

Krusemark, Renne. *The Role of Critical Thinking in Reader Perceptions of Leadership in Comic Books.* PhD Dissertation, Creighton University, 2014.

Low, David E. "'Spaces Invested with Content': Crossing the 'Gaps' in Comics with Readers in Schools." *Children's Literature in Education: An International Quarterly,* vol. 43, no. 4, 2012, pp. 368–385.

Maynard, Amy. "How Comics Help to Teach Shakespeare in Schools." *Asiatic: IIUM Journal of English Language and Literature (AsiaticI)*, vol. 6, no. 2, Dec. 2012, pp. 96–109.

Round, Julia. *Gothic in Comics and Graphic Novels: A Critical Approach.* McFarland, 2014.

Sabeti, Shari. "The 'Strange Alteration' of Hamlet: Comic Books, Adaptation, and Constructions of Adolescent Literacy." *Changing English,* vol. 21, no. 2, 2014, pp. 182–197.

Schroeder, Andrew F. *Instruction of the Innocent: Comics as Curriculum.* PhD Dissertation, Roosevelt University, 2015.

Stevenson, Robert Louis. *Strange Case of Dr. Jekyll and Mr. Hyde*, Norton Critical Ed., edited by Katherine Linehan. W.W. Norton and Company, 2003 (1886).

Wainer, Alex. *Soul of the Dark Knight: Batman as Mythic Figure in Comics and Film.* McFarland, 2014.

PART III

Graphic Novels, Empathy, and Social Engagement

CHAPTER 9

Teaching *March* in the Borderlands between Social Justice and Pop Culture

Susanna Hoeness-Krupsaw

The recent publication of Georgia Congressman John Lewis's three-volume graphic memoir, *March*, permits instructors of many different types of courses to introduce their students to current political and historical events through an attractively laid out graphic medium, which, as Scott McCloud suggests, can amplify a topic by simplifying it (30). With this hybrid pop culture medium positioned in the "borderlands" between text and picture, students can easily be led to a greater understanding of various aspects and key events of the Civil Rights Movement, while simultaneously honing their empathic capacity.[1]

Instrumental in procuring civil rights for African Americans in the 1960s, John Lewis deplores the relative ignorance of the younger generation concerning this important chapter in American history. In a recent article in *American History*, Gene Semour asked, "How do you tell this often forgotten story to a new generation?" (27). John Lewis intended his graphic memoir to answer this question in no uncertain terms, saying "I think the book to some degree has become what I like to call a change agent ... [that] has caused another generation to get out there and push and pull and try to set things right" (qtd. in Gustines). By imbuing its main character with the qualities of a superhero, involving readers emotionally in history and making complicated political processes visually explicit, as well as exhibiting excellent

S. Hoeness-Krupsaw (✉)
University of Southern Indiana, Evansville, IN, USA

© The Author(s) 2018
A. Burger (ed.), *Teaching Graphic Novels in the English Classroom*,
DOI 10.1007/978-3-319-63459-3_9

artistic quality, this graphic narrative is supremely capable of eliciting the empathy needed to embrace and care about social justice issues.

According to *New York Times* author George Gustines, the idea for Lewis's narrative originated in a slim comic titled *Martin Luther King and the Montgomery Story*, which was published in 1957 and promoted non-violent civil disobedience. When Lewis and Andrew Aydin, Lewis's digital director and policy adviser, talked about the King comic in 2008, they discovered how influential this book, about which Aydin had written a master's thesis, had been for Lewis. The little comic book, produced by Alfred Hassler of the Fellowship of Reconciliation, included a procedure for implementing the Montgomery Method that still exerts its influence today. In *Across that Bridge*, Lewis, an admirer of the protesters in Tahrir Square, mentions that an Arabic translation of the comic was distributed to Egyptian demonstrators to instruct them in methods of non-violent resistance (83). Eventually, Aydin suggested collaboration on a graphic memoir detailing key stages of Lewis's career.

Civil Rights Superheroes

If Dr. King appears as a superhero in *The Montgomery Story*, it is safe to say that so does John Lewis in *March*. The graphic narrative format of Lewis's memoir caters to our students' already existing excitement about and understanding of American superhero comics. Despite the realistic historical setting of the narrative and elements of characterization as well as identity formation, Lewis is also elevated to mythic levels while still remaining human and relatable. His journey from inauspicious beginnings in rural Alabama, experiencing poverty and discrimination, to the civil rights era battles, to political power and social influence, retraces the stages of the traditional heroic quest. Like any mythic hero, Lewis experiences a threshold call to action when he hears Dr. King speak on the radio. He undergoes a series of tests, with the beatings at Selma perhaps illustrating the most desperate point of his struggles, what Joseph Campbell describes as the "Whale's belly" stage (245), only to return after these adventures with the boon of wisdom and righteousness that will allow him to become a political leader and spokesperson.

Authors Doug Sandler and Robin Rosenberg agree that, despite their extraordinary powers, superheroes' ordinary characteristics have the ability to inspire us to take action. In his brief *Huffington Post* article, Sandler gives our students a very accessible outline for the discussion of John Lewis as a down-to-earth superhero. We look up to superheroes because they have weaknesses that they confront, archenemies who stand in their way, goals that give their life purpose. They pursue these goals with great tenacity, and never abandon their dreams. After reading *March*, students should have no trouble at all finding strong examples of these characteristics in Mr. Lewis's life story. They will find Lewis's convictions inspirational and transformative: "All our work, all our struggle, all our days add up to one purpose: to reconcile ourselves to the truth, and finally accept once and for all that we are one people, one family, the human family, that we are all emanations of one divine source, that source is Love" (Lewis and Jones 177). Rosenberg reiterates that these powerful superhero narratives "tap into our capacity for empathy." It is easy to see how the ordinary man, John Lewis, makes us feel his extraordinary passion for justice.

Empathic Responses

Multisensory experience makes a graphic narrative like *March* uniquely capable of reaching out to our students, particularly those who have difficulty imagining vivid scenes on their own or those who struggle with longer, more complex, print texts. As Lewis himself writes in Book Three, "A Movement is fueled by passion" (92). Such passion may be singularly capable of eliciting the kind of feeling that can evoke empathy, the absence of which various different commentators have recently deplored.

In *Across that Bridge*, Lewis mentions that he notices how young people today do not understand very well "how we could have taken what seems to them to be such illogical steps in the fight for freedom" (165). Gail Rebuck, chair of Random House UK, reported in the *Guardian* in 2011 on the decline of empathic behaviors among teenagers and heavy digital device users. The exact reasons are not known yet, but many observers blame technology and offer reading as a solution. Rebuck writes, "The research shows that if we stop reading, we will be different people: less intricate, less empathetic, less interesting. There can hardly be a better reason for fighting to protect the future of the book." Robert Dilenschneider, writing for the University of Pittsburgh's leadership journal *Leader to Leader*, also deplored the deterioration of basic rules of politeness in public discourse and interactions. Sue Shellenbarger in the *Wall Street Journal* observes that, with the teenage brain still developing, 13–16-year old boys might actually experience a decline in empathic behaviors. Since this age group is also a prime audience for cartoons, a book that can create passion and empathy recommends itself as a reading selection aimed at enhancing students' empathetic responses to social justice issues.

To combat the apathy noted above, we can make use of powerful stories like Congressman Lewis's *March*. Many contemporary philosophers and psychologists agree that our feelings produce the kind of empathy requisite for moral judgments and ethical behaviors (Gerreck 96). In the Western tradition, we often regard Socrates, Plato, and Aristotle as the ancients who showed us a path toward the good life, but the thinkers of the Scottish Enlightenment were early forerunners of a type of thinking that has garnered attention in moral philosophy and psychology, as well as cognitive science and neuroscience.[2] They affirmed that we are born with a good amount of what they called "benevolence," which is an interest in others' well-being. Hence, they claimed, we are born with a moral sense faculty, an innate sense of moral values cultivated through our interactions with others (Mower et al. 2).

Ethicist Monica Gerreck describes the imaginary work necessary to empathize as follows: "Sympathy enables us to get inside the experience of others by *imagining* ourselves in their situation" (97, emphasis added). Adam Smith employed the construct of the "impartial spectator" to explain the rational processes that follow emotional responses (Gerreck 99). Most importantly, the Scottish Enlightenment philosophers (not just Smith, but also David Hume and Frances Hutcheson, despite variances in their respective terminology) insisted on the "spectator perspective" because they saw "being human and having an idea of morality at all" as being predicated on our relationships with others (Mower et al. 8). The three Scottish thinkers also agreed on our ability to educate the "internal spectator" through habit and on the resulting happiness (Gerreck 103). The implications for our classes are clear: if we can involve our students emotionally, we can increase their empathy, thus fostering the habits of moral judgment propounded by the Scottish Enlightenment and confirmed by cognitive and neuroscience research today.

Indeed, the Sentimentalists' hunches are now supported by MRIs and other experiments in neuroscience, revealing a *dual process model* that includes aesthetic reactions as part of a network of affective responses tied intimately to evaluative judgments that trigger moral reasoning (Lapsley). The latest Theory of Mind (ToM) supports the idea that cognition requires the kind of affective, empathic responses stimulated by our literature courses, which can thus serve as a training ground for our students' sensibilities, guiding them toward making morally astute decisions, as well as practicing the logical thinking needed in business and science. The process essentially delineates the same mechanism suggested by the Sentimentalists: emotional involvement comes first, followed by empathic response, which is then cognitively evaluated.

Cognitive scientists now give us clever scientific answers to questions we have always been able to answer intuitively. They find that we can infer mental states not just from observing people's body language directly but from reading about it. This type of research throws an interesting light on the skills we acquire from reading. Recent theories of embodied cognition explain how we process emotional information. The findings indicate that thinking about and imagining an experience activates similar brain functions to when we are actually experiencing it. David Comer Kidd and Emanuele Castano were able to show a connection between reading fiction, self-reported empathy, and performance on an advanced affective ToM test (377).

Social psychologists John Dovidio, Anja Eller, and Miles Hewstone were able to show that studying literary texts improved intergroup relations because fiction offers an abstraction and simulation of social experience. It is the reader's access to characters' inner lives that makes literary fiction a particularly valuable tool for learning how to interpret the unexpected and unknown. This means that even indirect—imagined—contact is nearly as valuable as direct contact with members of other groups, something amply illustrated in the research completed by Johnson et al. when they found that reading narrative fiction changed individuals' race boundary perceptions in experiments that involved testing race bias in photo selections. In sum, exposure to carefully selected fiction reduced thinking in biased categories.

Through cognitive monitoring of our responses to fictional situations, we can learn about life. In a study of the effects narrative fiction has on readers, Raymond Mar and Keith Oatley see stories as "social guides." Especially instructive are realistic novels that feature strong interpersonal relationships (Mar and Oatley 185) and "challenging" plot lines that require attention and some effort at interpretation. They posit that "the multisensory narrative portrayals in theater, film, and television may be especially useful for learning how to decode subtle nonverbal clues" (Mar and Oatley 186). Such findings place additional value on the multisensory elements in graphic narratives like *March*.

For instructors wishing to connect artistic and literary experiences, graphic narratives offer many options, even for the most reluctant readers, because the visual medium focuses readers' attention differently than does text alone. Catherine Elgin, whose work examines the philosophy of knowledge, regards emotion as just a facet of reason that provides an avenue of access to other, more scientific, types of knowledge (33). Emotions, she argues, provide sources of salience. These are fixed patterns of attention highlighting certain features of one domain and obscuring others (Elgin 43). Researchers remark on the importance of "attention" in the processing of aesthetic experiences because it enhances cognition.

March offers both historical narrative and engagement in the visual representation of John Lewis's civil rights struggles and thus produces a visceral experience that creates curiosity about recent historical events and spurs thoughtful discussion about current social issues. Monika Fludernik's article on cognitive processing points out that blends "in cognitive studies refer to conceptual overlay; a functional joining of two 'mental spaces' that helps to create innovative meaning potential and facilitates mental reorientation." Such recent research in cognition and linguistics suggests the enormous potential of graphic narratives such as *March* in creating additional signification beyond the written word and the image in the third new space that arises from the blending of text and image. In this hybrid space, Congressman Lewis's narrative will inspire our students' critical and empathic abilities.

Visual Aesthetics

Readers will immediately notice the excellent quality of the visual presentation in all three volumes of the *March* trilogy. Drawn by bestselling graphic novelist Nate Powell, the graphic art has been deemed of the highest quality by all reviewers, even those who tend to doubt the ability of non-fiction graphic narratives to portray historical events accurately or appropriately. Readers may be familiar with some of Powell's other publications, including his award-winning teen novel *Swallow Me Whole*.

The strength of Powell's art in *March* relies on his use of black and white, rather than color, drawings. As Jan Baetens points out, it is clearly more economical not to print in color (111). As we can see in other black and white narratives, such as Marjane Satrapi's *Persepolis* (2007), the technique evokes the more critically acclaimed low-scale graphic narrative productions as opposed to the large-scale mass-market color comics productions (Baetens 112). Critics, however, rarely comment on color, perhaps because, in our text-based field, the color of print plays a minor role. Perhaps Powell's use of a black and white scheme has more to do with evoking the "color" of John Lewis's memories. In times so tension-laden as the 1950s and 1960s, the camps were clearly pitched on either side of the fight for civil rights; issues were truly seen as black and white.

Moreover, this more serious black and white presentation is able to evoke the impression given by newsreels or TV documentaries from the 1950s and early 1960s, many of which would also still be mostly just in black and white, as color televisions did not become available until about 1954. In this context, it could be argued, by my logic, that the frame narrative presented in the novel's opening pages, for instance, should be in color. I think, however, that this mechanism would have disrupted the artistic impression of the narrative as a whole. Eliminating the color inking by yet another artist or a whole group of assembly line workers also gave Powell more control over his work (Baetens 115). Baetens emphasizes that, despite the availability of "direct color," sophisticated artists prefer "personality and attitude" to colorization and cuteness (116). In a medium that emphasizes drawing and color, color is only required when it helps the reader understand the fictional world better (Baetens 117). In Lewis's piece, that is clearly not the case: we understand without the assistance of colorful sketching.

These distinctions between the black and white and color medium can be used in preparatory discussions before students begin reading the graphic narrative itself. Many will have some experience with superhero comics, almost all of them in color reproductions, or with superhero-style video games. An interesting discussion can elicit comments on their own aesthetic preferences. By contrasting images from Dr. King's readily available *The Montgomery Story* with any of the pages in *March*, students can be asked to assess their impressions. Which style is more aesthetically pleasing, memorable, impressive, or costly to reproduce?

Other aesthetic concerns can be addressed through the book's introductory pages. Starting Book One in medias res, before the actual opening of the novel, readers are immediately invited into the story by joining the marchers on Edmund Pettus Bridge in Selma (5). Eschewing the traditional six-or-eight-panel layout, Powell uses the varying panel sizes to create an eye-catching viewing experience. He contrasts the distant glimpse of bridge and marchers with a close-up of two black men worried about having to jump off the bridge to escape the violence, suggested in a wordless panel featuring two helmeted police or National Guard officers. The threat is powerfully confirmed by showing only two hands desperately trying to grasp firm ground, transitioning then to complete blackness (9). Through examples such as these, students of all ages can be invited to describe the emotional impact of these visual elements on their reading experience.

Further, Congressman Lewis's memoir permits sophisticated analysis of the uses of frame narratives. Set at the time of President Barack Obama's inauguration in January 2009, the opening pages of Book One raise the expectations of a contemporary reflection that suddenly flashes back some 50 years. We can study the purpose and effects of the novel's frame narrative, the use of which both puzzles and intrigues students. George G. Gustine's article sheds some light on the reasoning behind the framing mechanism when he quotes Mr. Lewis as saying, "I was there and I wondered: 'How could people be so mean and vicious? How could this happen?'" Thus, the graphic narrative creates a visual contrast between the celebratory moments at President Obama's inauguration and the violence of the Bloody Sunday events. Student readers will realize that the counterpointing of past and present in this manner produces in the reader a kind of analogical thinking that permits both a comparing and contrasting of events (something social studies instructors can pursue in class assignments) and a gauging of historical progress from marching for civil rights to inaugurating the first black American president.

Given the memory work this novel has to accomplish, the majority of the narrative occurs through flashback. That is, in itself, not unusual, but can lead to a number of different discussion points such as the reliability of memory, the reliability of the first-person narrator, and our assessments of print versus pictorial memories. Lewis's co-author Andrew Aydin reports conducting detailed fact-checking to verify Lewis's recollections of events that occurred 60 years before (Seymour 31). A brief reflection exercise on weekend activities among a group of students will reveal not only divergent recollections of the same events but also vastly different assessments of these events' significance. This should sufficiently illustrate our difficulties in reconstructing the past.

A comparative analysis of one particular memory and its representation in three different media will further illustrate the point. Lewis's recollecting his affections for his parents' chickens, and his preaching to them, takes up a couple of pages in his *Walking with the Wind: A Memoir of the Movement* (39–40). It becomes, however, the central concern of a recent children's book by Jabari Asim. Asim illustrates the incident in vivid but sketchy imagery well-suited to a younger reading audience. Text and picture book can then be viewed in conjunction with the graphic narrative to further illustrate our special reading strategies for the graphic narrative medium.

Proverbially, "pictures do not lie," hence what we see tends to strike us as more authentic than something we hear or read. Much work has been done by Marianne Hirsch and others in the arena of memory studies, exploring how traumatic memories are transmitted from generation to generation, and what role photos play in the process of pictorially constructed memories. Hirsch began her book *Family Frames* with an analysis of the use of drawn versions of photos in Art Spiegelman's *Maus* to trigger active recollection, what she calls "postmemory" (13). Like Lewis, Hirsch believes in the importance of recovering such memories to preserve them for posterity. Thus, her scholarship has become for her a kind of activism (Hirsch 13). Hirsch remarks on the representational quality of photos that are supremely capable of evoking feelings and associated memories within us, which explains why Spiegelman would intersperse drawn versions of photos in his graphic narratives (Hirsch 37). Instructors interested in pursuing a more detailed analysis of the similarities and differences between viewing a photographic record of the events at Selma, for instance, and reading the graphic narrative can project selected pages from Gene Seymour's article in *American History*, in which he counterpoints specific scenes in the graphic narrative and matching photographic footage.[3]

Instructors can make Lewis's narrative even more immediate and pertinent to their students through connections to recently successful popular movies, such as *Selma, The Butler,* and *The Help*, permitting reflection on content and genre similarities and differences.

An early review article in *Publisher's Weekly* described Nate Powell's illustrations as "cinematic" because his "powerful art eschews gentle shading for sharp lines and inky black pools that frame the emotional context, though they sometimes fail to properly distinguish the characters" ("You Don't Say"). One can easily illustrate this assessment by studying the opening pages of Book One of *March*. A slow zooming in on the setting in Washington, DC on January 20, 2009, featuring, first, Lewis's street during the early morning hours, followed by a glimpse of the staircase, framed pictures along its walls, and then a slow approach into Lewis's bedroom offers yet another example of Powell's film-like representation of this moment (Lewis et al. 12).[4]

It is worth pointing out here, however, that McCloud wants us to distinguish very carefully between movies and comics. He adamantly maintains careful distinctions that students can be made to appreciate when we watch a movie, stop the movie, and try to discuss details without rewinding and reviewing. We have to rely on our recollections because, as he emphasizes, the movie is "sequential in time" (McCloud 7). Conversely, we can see an entire series of actions all at once when the graphic narrative is open before us, because it is "spatially juxtaposed" (ibid.). This is, of course, another good moment to present the students with the uses of the gutter. Where our movie sequence lets us see every detail unfolding in front of our eyes, the graphic narrative operates with a limited series of panel images, the gutter inviting us to fill the gap with our own thoughts, inferences, and imagination.

Indeed, Lewis's narrative illustrates a sophisticated handling of time: the frame narrative moves to his memories via the chicken images a group of visitors admire in his office. Suddenly the use of the frame narrative becomes clear. While creating historical pertinence, it also permits a smooth intro-duction of recollections. We can see how the graphic medium sharpens students' reading skills with flashbacks, symbolism, and provocative visual style choices. For instance, exploration of selected story frames reveals the sophisticated handling of time through the visual medium. More "inky black pools" occur, for instance, when Lewis recalls his childhood reading of the Bible and his incomprehension of one particular verse. This preoc-cupation is powerfully rendered by inscribing the verse on the boy's body. The pages showing young John preaching to the chickens is kept entirely in black, revealing both the darkness of the hen house and perhaps also his fears of trespassing against the commandments of peacefulness and charity that influenced him so strongly during his formative years (Lewis et al. 27–29). In such "bleeds," a term McCloud uses for pages with open-ended panels, time spills over into "timeless space" (103) and evokes the lasting impact these memories had on Lewis.

With the help of this novel, students can study nearly all of the visual elements introduced in McCloud's seminal work *Understanding Comics*. For instance, "the jagged staccato rhythm of unconnected moments" (McCloud 67) can be illustrated with sequential panels that let us move swiftly through several key moments. It is clear to us that time and distance have elapsed between the frames showing young John in bed thinking and dreaming. Then Brown vs. the Board of Education is struck down a second time, and a brief authorial intrusion orients us to the death of Emmett Till that goes unpunished (Lewis et al. 56). No further explanation is neces-sary—we understand that, in these difficult times, John is still uncertain as to his future actions.

"Revelation of emotions," another key component in McCloud's work (118), is aptly handled through Powell's careful drawing. The previously mentioned hand attempting to grip the pavement on the Pettus Bridge wordlessly conveys the tension and fright experienced in this moment of violence (Lewis et al. 9). Another vivid example occurs when young John travels for the first time with his uncle from their home in the South to visit relatives in New York. While John's face expresses deep attention to the details of the trip, his uncle's face conveys worries (Lewis et al. 38). The next panel subtly suggests the reason for his facial expression. They may encounter violence and obstacles along the way, as evidenced in the frowns and scowls exhibited by the men at the rest stop. The same pages also illustrate well Powell's handling of space and motion by way of supplying road signs and cars. Students can be asked to identify the means by which the artist is able to suggest what is happening in the narrative without further explanation, and they can hone their critical-thinking skills by learning how to infer meaning from visual suggestions.

CONCLUSION

Through its pop culture superhero comics appeal, emotional impact, and aesthetically successful presentation, John Lewis's *March* makes a solid contribution to any classroom. It has already significantly impacted students across the country, as Gustines reports in the *New York Times*. Lewis's hopes that schools and universities would eventually use the book as a classroom text to allow students to "study and understand" (Gustines) the Civil Rights Movement and its emphasis on civil disobedience are being realized in various places: the New York City Department of Education is using *March* in a social studies program for eighth graders. Michigan State University, Georgia State University, and the University of Utah are using the text in reading programs (Gustines). Another hopeful example is related by Senator Lewis's co-author Andrew Aydin about the son of a *Wall Street Journal* reporter, who, after his father had given him the graphic narrative, put on his good clothes and paraded up and down, asking for equality. Aydin raises an evocative question, couched in hope for the future: "Imagine if we could instill a social consciousness in every 9-year-old in America. What would that do in a generation?" (qtd. in Gustines).

NOTES

1. "A Free Teacher's Guide to *March*" is available at http://www.topshelfcomix.com/contact/teachers-guide

2. This part of my article has been made possible in part by the 2016 National Endowment for the Humanities Summer Institute *Moral Psychology and Education: Putting the Humanities to Work*. Any views, findings, conclusions, or recommendations expressed in this article do not necessarily represent those of the National Endowment for the Humanities.
3. Photos can also be found at http://www.pbs.org/newshour/rundown/pho tos-selma-alabama-now/ and http://www.smithsonianmag.com/history/ rare-photos-selma-march-thick-history-180953874/
4. Unless otherwise noted, all references are to Book One of *March*.

WORKS CITED

Asim, Jabari. *Preaching to the Chickens: The Story of Young John Lewis*. Nancy Paulsen Books, 2016.

Baetens, Jan. "From Black & White to Color and Back: What Does It Mean (Not) to Use Color?" *College Literature*, vol. 38, Johns Hopkins University Press, 2011, pp. 111–128.

Brattico, Elvira and Pearce, Marcus. "The Neuroaesthetics of Music" *Psychology of Aesthetics,Creativity, and the Arts*, vol.7, no.1, 2013, pp. 48–61.

Campbell, Joseph. *The Hero with a Thousand Faces*, Bollingen Series XVII, 2nd ed. Princeton University Press, 1968.

Dilenschneider, Robert L. "Elevating Our Standards for Civility Leadership." *Leader to Leader* 67, Winter 2013, pp. 7–12, onlinelibrary.wiley.com/doi /10.1002/ltl.20055/full

Dovidio, John, Anja Eller, and Miles Hewstone. "Improving Intergroup Relations." *Group Processes and Intergroup Relations*, vol. 14, no.2, Mar. 2011, pp.147–160.

Elgin, Catherine Z. "Emotion and Understanding." *Epistemology and Emotions*, edited by George Brun, Ulvi Doğuoğlu, and Dominique Kuenzle, Routledge, 2008, pp. 33–50.

Fludernik, Monika. "Blending in Cartoons: The Production of Comedy." *Oxford Handbooks Online*. Oxford University Press, 2015.

Gerreck, Monica. "Revisiting Sentimentalism: A Smithian Normative Moral Theory." *New Essays on Adam Smith's Moral Philosophy*, edited by W. Robinson and D.B. Suits, RIT Press, 2012, pp. 95–104.

Gustines, George G. "At School, a 'March' through the Civil Rights Movement in ViDetail." *New York Times*, Aug 02, 2016, https://www.nytimes.com /2016/08/02/books/for-younger-readers-march-revisits-civil-rights-movement-in-visual-detail.html?_r=0

Hirsch, Marianne. *The Generation of Postmemory: Writing and Visual Culture After the Holocaust*. Columbia University Press, 2012.

Johnson, Dan R., Brandie L. Huffman, and Danny M. Jasper. "Changing Race Boundary Perception by Reading Narrative Fiction." *Basic And Applied Social*

Psychology, vol. 36, no. 1, 2014, pp. 83–90. EBSCOhost, doi: 10.1080/ 01973533.2013.856791

Kidd, David Comer, and Emanuele Castano. "Reading Literary Fiction Improves Theory of Mind." *Science*, vol 342, no. 6156, 3 Oct. 2013, pp. 377–380.

Lapsley, Daniel K., and Patrick L. Hill. "On Dual Processing and Heuristic Approaches to Moral Cognition." *Journal of Moral Education*, vol. 37, no. 3, Sept. 2008, pp. 313–332. Academic Search Premier, doi: 10.1080/ 03057240802227486

Lewis, John, Andrew Aydin, and Nate Powell. *March*, Book 1. Top Shelf, 2013

———. *March*, Book 2. Top Shelf, 2015.

———. *March*, Book 3. Top Shelf, 206.

Lewis, John with Brenda Jones. *Across the Bridge: Life Lessons and a Vision for Change*. Hyperion, 2012.

Lewis, John with Michael D'Orso. *Walking with the Wind: A Memoir of the Movement*. Simon and Schuster, 1998.

Martin Luther King, Jr. *The Montgomery Story*. Fellowship of Reconciliation, 1957, http://www.crmvet.org/docs/ms_for_comic.pdf

Mar, Raymond and Keith Oatley, "The Function of Fiction is the Abstraction and Simulation of Social Experience," *Perspectives on Psychological Science*, Vol. 3, 2008, pp. 173–192.

McCloud, Scott. *Understanding Comics: The Invisible Art*. HarperPerennial, 1994.

"You Don't Say: Stories, 2004–2013." *Publisher's Weekly*, n.d., http://www.publi shersweekly.com/978-1-6030-9366-8

Mower, Deborah, Wade L. Robinson, and Phyllis Vandenberg. "Reintroducing Moral Sensitivity." *Developing Moral Sensitivity*, edited by Deborah Mower, Wade L. Robison, and Phyllis Vandenberg, Routledge, 2015, pp. 1–14.

Rebuck Gail, "Humans Have the Need to Read." *The Guardian (US Edition)*, 30 Dec. 2011. https://www.theguardian.com/commentisfree/2011/dec/30/humans-hardwired-read-books

Rosenberg, Robin. "The Psychology Behind Superhero Origin Stories." *Smithsonian Magazine*, February 2013, http://www.smithsonianmag.com/a rts-culture/the-psychology-behind-superhero-origin-stories-4015776/

Sandler, Doug. "5 Lessons Superheroes Teach Us About Life." *The Huffington Post*, 29 October 2015, http://www.huffingtonpost.com/doug-a-sandler/lessons-superheroes_b_8387272.html

Seymour, Gene. "The Graphic Life of John Lewis." *American History*, vol. 50, no. 5, 12, 2015, pp. 26–35.

Shellenbarger, Sue. "Teens Are Still Developing Empathy Skills." *The Wall Street Journal Online*, 15 October 2013, http://www.wsj.com/articles/ SB10001424052702304561004579137514122387441

Revising the Rhetoric of "Boat People" through the Interactive Graphic Adaptation of Nam Le's "The Boat"

Jennifer Phillips

Literature has been shown to have the power to increase empathy in readers (Mar et al. 694).[1] As teachers of literature, we hope not only to demonstrate the ways in which this process occurs, but also train our students to be more empathic, more open, more aware of the world outside of the text that the text itself illuminates, or by which it is illuminated. In a world of increasing access to information, where the vast majority of our students carry smartphones with instant access to the far reaches of the internet, we teachers face a tension between increasing student knowledge and decreasing student discernment. Moreover, it has been shown that access to this amount of information actually has the effect of decreasing empathy, rather than increasing it (Konrath et al. 180).

In this chapter, I will examine some of the issues facing teachers of literature as we present students with texts that engage with current global issues—in this instance, the Global Migration Crisis. After outlining these issues, I will show how literature can be used to mitigate apathy produced by information overload, statistical numbing, and false constructions based on political

J. Phillips (✉)
Wuhan University, Wuhan, China

The University of Wollongong, Wollongong, NSW, Australia

© The Author(s) 2018
A. Burger (ed.), *Teaching Graphic Novels in the English Classroom,*
DOI 10.1007/978-3-319-63459-3_10

149

rhetoric and discourses. Moreover, I will demonstrate how graphic adaptations of literature—or more generally, graphic novels and interactive graphic adventures—are even more effective than literature in creating the empathy necessary to break through some of the inertia of the internet age. I will do so through an analysis of the online graphic adaptation of Nam Le's short story "The Boat."

NAM LE'S *THE BOAT*

In 2007, Nam Le published his story "The Boat" as the final entry in his first collection of short stories. The collection, also entitled *The Boat*, was the first in a trend of Australian Transnational writing. The diversity of subject matter—including a struggling Australian writer living in America, a Columbian drug cartel, and a Hiroshima survivor, among others—reflects the new global reality, or, more accurately, a global literary interconnectedness. This transnational trend in Australian literature has manifested more recently in other collections of short stories such as Ali Alizadeh's *Transactions* (2013) and Maxine Beneba Clarke's *Foreign Soil* (2014).

Yet despite the global reach of Le's subject matter, most reviewers and critics focused on the collection's opening and closing stories and the way they reflect Le's own experience as a refugee who traveled with his parents by boat from Vietnam to Australia. While I acknowledge that there is much that still needs to be said about the global reach of Le's writing, and transnational Australian literature in general, in this chapter I want to demonstrate that there is strength in allowing the fiction/memoir byplay in the opening and closing stories of Le's collection to influence the readers' interpretation. Moreover, in what follows, I want to present a way that reading Nam Le's work—particularly the titular short story "The Boat," alongside the online graphic adaptation of the story by Matt Hyunh (accessible at sbs.com.au/theboat)—contributes to a process of affect that is an essential counterbalance to the problem of apathy and ignorance evident in the many popular misunderstandings of refugee experiences.

REFUGEES: THE GLOBAL CONTEXT

When teaching a text like "The Boat," it is necessary to situate it within the current global context, as well as the context in which it was written. In the case of this text, the events which have been taking place since summer 2015, particularly in Europe, cannot be ignored. It is no exaggeration to say that the world is in the midst of the largest displacement and resettlement of people in over 25 years (according to the International Rescue Committee). In September 2016, it was estimated that 11 million Syrian nationals had been made homeless by their country's civil war, with 4 million of them seeking refuge outside of the country (UNHCR, "Syria Fact Sheet"). In addition to Syria, the majority of refugees are fleeing Afghanistan and Somalia (UNHCR, "Figures at a Glance"). Globally, this figure is much higher, with internally displaced refugees numbering 34 million in 2015, and the total number of refugees and asylum seekers reaching 20.2 million in that same year (Zarracina). The most recent United Nations High Commissioner for Refugees (UNHCR) statistics place the total figure of forcibly displaced persons at 65.3 million, 21.3 million of whom are refugees, a rate which is increasing by nearly 34,000 people per day ("Figures at a Glance").

Much has been said about the so-called "global refugee crisis," with opinions shared by people as diverse as politicians, aid agencies, and even actors. At one point Benedict Cumberbatch (best known for his role in BBC's *Sherlock*) was criticized among other British actors for using his star power to encourage fans to donate to the refugee crisis (Delingpole). So many statistics have been shared and so many op-eds penned that the average student would find it difficult to comprehend what a huge impact this global displacement has had. Yet what is more of a concern, as we, as teachers, try to educate our students, is that, in the haze of numbers and statistics, human suffering is overlooked; the human reality is lost.

Of course, at times a rare personal story is shared amidst the statistics, a human moment captured, and for that moment the world takes notice. Such was the effect of the images of three-year-old Alan Kurdi,[2] whose body washed ashore on a Turkish beach, his tiny shoes still on his feet. He drowned along with his mother and elder brother. Heartbroken, his surviving father returned to Syria to bury his family (Elgot). *Time* magazine dubbed the images "the most heartbreaking images of 2015," with the photographs going viral on social media and reported by countless international news agencies. Fueled by the public outrage, promises were soon made by the governments of Germany, the United Kingdom, Canada, and Australia, pledging to increase refugee intake. However, within one year of Kurdi's death, only Canada's promises had come to fruition (Costello).

A text like "The Boat" functions in a similar way to the personal affect created by the story of Alan Kurdi. However, where the challenge lies, for us as educators, is in not only communicating and applying the fictional world to the real world, but provoking change and action as a result—something the real story of the tragic death of Alan Kurdi failed to achieve.

REFUGEES: THE AUSTRALIAN CONTEXT

In what follows, I will consider the ways Australian public perception of refugees has been manipulated by the propagation of false or misleading facts and catchy (but constructed) slogans, repeated in various guises since their first appearance in the late 1970s. As such, much of the Australian voting public's reactions to the issue have been based on emotions which have no basis in fact.

In contrast to the scope and scale of global refugee statistics, Australia received only one boat arrival with 160 people in 2014 (2015 statistics have not been released at the time of this writing) (Phillips).[3] Yet, despite this, since 2001, sparked in part by 9/11 and the fear of global terrorism, there has been a growing discourse about Australia's intake of refugees, one which is part fact, part political propaganda, and part ignorant construction. Within these debates, as we will see, the term "boat people" has been used not only to denote the mode of transportation used by those hoping to gain asylum in Australia, but to dehumanize and objectify them, thus triggering statistical numbing, or to create an image distorted from reality and robbing the Australian people of the reasoned analysis necessary for effective and practical affective behavior.

The term "boat people" was first used in Australian political discourse in the late 1970s. Although no one can pinpoint precisely when the term originated, its use coincided with the federal election campaign of that year. The triggering event was the arrival in Darwin, in Australia's Northern Territory, of six boats carrying 218 refugees fleeing Vietnam (Neumann). The 1977 incident established many of the patterns within the political discourse to follow. The fear of opening the floodgates would be invoked countless times in political and media discourse in Australia, used most recently by Malcolm Turnbull, the current Australian Prime Minister, in an interview in February 2016 (McMah). The phrase "illegal immigrants" would be used by both parties in the 2013 and 2016 elections, despite the fact there is debate about the illegal nature of such an act.[4] Additionally, the term "queue jumping," introduced in 1977, is an accepted part of the Australian vernacular used to deride and denigrate asylum seekers, despite the fact that there is no such queue to jump (Tickner).

The most recent developments in the asylum-seeker debates in Australia have revolved around the treatment of those who have already arrived and are waiting for their claims to be processed. In August 2016, a slew of 2,000 documents, totaling over 8,000 pages, were leaked. These papers revealed horrific conditions in an offshore detention center on the island of Nauru, which is part of Australia's mandatory offshore detention program for asylum seekers. Stories included guards allegedly grabbing young boys and threatening to kill them and a young girl given an additional two-minute shower, but only after the performance of sexual acts for guards. There were also reports of incidents of abuse of children at the hands of other detainees (Farrell et al.).

Perhaps the greatest tragedy of these revelations is that, despite the slick graphics employed by the *Guardian* website to communicate these horrors, very little has been done in response to these explosive claims.

Impossible Empathy?

One of the key issues with teaching a text which raises these issues in the Australian context, as well as globally, is not only the global information fatigue, but the inability to sort fiction from fact. In the face of these horrific statistics and events, there is a feeling of hopelessness or even apathy. Our students, even those sympathetic to the suffering of the struggling, lost, homeless, and stateless, may not have the skills or abilities to make informed decisions and take appropriate actions in response. They are not alone. Numerous studies have been conducted on the phenomenon known as "statistical numbing." Essentially, this is the curious effect behind Joseph Stalin's infamous claim, namely, that "the death of one man is a tragedy, the death of millions is a statistic."[5] This is the reason why the large numbers and statistics of the Nauru papers are far less emotionally affecting than the tragic story of Alan Kurdi.

One reason for this disconnection may be that, as Paul Slovic observes, "numerical representations of human lives do not necessarily convey the importance of those lives." Slovic argues that statistics fail to produce affect, which he defines as "the positive and negative feelings that combine with reasoned analysis to guide our judgments, decisions, and actions." Key to motivating action, Slovic claims, is feeling. Feeling triggers analysis, which results in action. Thus, when presented with data such as the number of people displaced, the number of deaths at sea, or the number of people who have died in these war-torn regions without even having the chance to seek asylum, these numbers are not powerful enough to create the emotional response necessary to begin the affect process Slovic outlines. The lack of an emotional response leads to a failure on the part of the individual to make a reasoned analysis and, as a result, no action is taken.

Studies have shown that affect increases when the stimulus of emotion is personified, rather than objectified. Loran F. Nordgren and Mary-Hunter Morris McDonnell found that the personification of the injured produces a greater process of affect, facilitating the emotional response, triggering an analysis of the situation, and causing a resulting action. They called this the "victim identifiability effect" (97). However, where Nordgren and McDonnell found that the inclusion of an emotional trigger (such as the victim's photograph) increased the emotional response and therefore the affective reaction of the participants, Deborah Small, Paul Slovic, and George Lowenstein found the opposite to be the case: in an experiment in which the inclusion of an image of an African girl in need was presented alongside statistics showing the number of African people in need, the number of donations decreased (Small et al. 151).

Slovic believes that key to the process of creating empathy and identification is to cultivate attention. A similar discovery was made by Paul Zak at UC Berkeley, whose study uncovered that when we hear an affective story (which he defines as one that has the power to hold our attention as well as transport us into the characters' worlds), the amount of oxytocin in our brains increases. Interestingly, oxytocin is the same chemical responsible for empathy. Therefore, if full attention is given to the individual, the emotional connection grows, leading to empathy as well as the process of affective decision-making.

Conversely, if the attention is split, such as between the individual story and the statistic, as seen in the study by Small, Slovic, and Lowenstein, the additional information dilutes the consumer's attention span and dulls the emotional connection. Thus, it is the emotional connection through story that is key to this process. Perhaps it is the lack of attention given to online forms of reading, statistically more likely to take place on smartphones ("Internet Stats & Facts for 2016"), that also dulls the formation of empathy. Moreover, the form in which this information is found also impacts students' response to it.

To counteract the effects of political discourses, as well as the statistical numbness that comes from revelations such as those which came from Nauru, I propose a move away from statistics, a move away from arguments about political structures and responses, and instead a move into the world of narrative in order to break down prejudices and misunderstandings about the experience of refugees. I propose an analysis of the affective impact not only of personal story (as seen in Nam Le's short story "The Boat"), but of the greater empathy which can be created by comic form (as seen in the online graphic adaptation of "The Boat"). With these approaches in mind, I will argue that the seeds of empathy planted by the autobiographical short story are harvested through the affective and immersive nature of the interactive website.

Stories: Affect beyond Statistics, Rhetoric, and Politics

Just as narrative fiction has been shown to increase empathy, so, too, studies have shown the link between the form of empathy created, an increase in the reader's social inclusion, and shifts in racial stereotyping (Johnson, Huffman, and Jasper 88). In what follows, I will consider the textual process which facilitates this process of empathy, and investigate if the graphic adaptation of a text expedites this process.

Nam Le's short story "The Boat" is the final short story in a collection of the same name. Thus, in naming the collection after this story, as well as bookending the collection with similar themes of the migrant experience, its importance to Le's communicative affect is highlighted. The opening story in Le's collection, "Love and Honour and Pity and Pride and Compassion and Sacrifice," depicts a writer, also named Nam, as he struggles with what he sees as an expectation to write an "ethnic story," because, as one character tells him, "Ethnic literature's hot. And important too." Although the real and fictional versions of Nam do eventually write about "Vietnamese boat people," only the "real" story remains, with the fictional version burned after it is read by Nam's dad.

Thus, the story "The Boat" is the "Vietnamese boat people" story which remains. By using the framing narrative to describe this final story as such, Le is pointing toward the "boat people" discourses in Australian (and perhaps global) political rhetoric. But throughout the text, he redeems the journey of "boat people," transforming it from a mere statistic, in danger of statistical numbing, as well as rewriting and reclaiming the term "boat people" as a badge of honor, rather than a term of political disdain.

The story "The Boat" depicts a horrific ocean crossing through the eyes of Mai, a young Vietnamese woman fleeing after her father has been captured and tortured in a re-education camp. In the crush of bodies, Mai befriends Quyen, an older woman, and her six-year-old son, Truong. The three band together and support each other through storms, sickness, and the ever-present threat of death. Over the course of the journey, Truong gets sicker and sicker until, tragically, he dies and is thrown overboard, a few scant miles before the boat reaches the Australian shore. Although not an autobiographical story, "The Boat" is informed by Nam Le's own experiences: Le's parents made a similar journey to Australia fleeing Vietnam, taking Le with them when he was only one year old (George).

Where we have seen that statistics, even of horrific events, often dehumanize and lead to numbness rather than an affective response, personal stories have the power to create empathy and empower affective connections. Throughout "The Boat," this process of humanizing takes place through personal characterization as well as visceral representations. Abjection is a key technique here. In the middle of a storm, faced with the stench of human vomit and excrement, Mai's stomach feels as if it is "forced up, squashed through her throat." So horrific is the experience for her that she considers it "the moment before death."

The physical reality of such a journey is made tangible through details: the wind running through the boat in a storm is described as a "chorus of low moans." Bodies "collide" and "slam" into one another, the crush of humanity becomes a mass of disembodied "thighs and ribs and arms and heads." There is an irony here, that one way to counter and correct the dehumanization of the "boat people" discourse is through the very same technique. Yet, in this context, focalized through the experience of Mai, the mass of "boat people" makes real the horrors of the journey.

The reality of the horrors depicted is an important part of creating empathy and breaking down political rhetoric. Australian political discourse has often painted "boat people" as "lazy," "queue-jumpers," or those who are choosing the "easy way" to Australia. In this story, the journey is shown to be anything but easy. When a storm hits the boat, Mai feels the "panicked pimps, people clawing for direction, sudden slaps of ice-cold water" as "the whole world reeled." The perilous nature of a journey on the open sea is clear here; it is not, as one Australian politician once put it, as easy as crossing Sydney Harbour on the Manly Ferry (Newman).

Where statistics and rhetoric have failed to accurately represent the lived experience of refugee migration, Le's story is able to capture this. Mai's only comfort in her journey is her connection to Quyen and her son, Truong. The three become a surrogate family, Quyen treating Mai like a daughter and Mai treating Truong like her own son. However, soon, this family unit is shattered. Faced with water and food shortages after the storm causes all of the onboard food to perish, they find themselves subsisting on only a few mouthfuls of food per day. Driven mad by thirst, Mai at one point drinks sea-water, only to have it cause a "raw scour of pain in her throat."

Mai survives, but Truong is not so fortunate. One morning, Mai discovers a "puddle of vomit next to his sleeping body," his eyes were "glazed" and "he looked like a burnt ghost." Truong hasn't made it through the night. Quyen wraps her young son's body in a blanket. From then, Truong is described only as a "bundle"; the life and humanity have departed from him. There is an additional irony in the use of depersonalization here. Instead of using such techniques to political ends in reducing empathy for "boat people," here, with his humanity taken away through death, Truong highlights the raw reality and perils of such a journey—that many who attempt it do not survive.

The ending of the story is apt. Mai and Quyen throw Truong's body overboard, just moments before the boat makes land. Rather than leaving the reader with an image of hope, or allowing them to dwell on the sad tragedy of Truong's loss, the last words highlight the indignity of Truong's death. Mai and Quyen throw him as far behind the boat as possible "so he would be out of sight when the sharks attacked." It is this image and the ignoble fate of Truong's body that close the text, as the reader is again introduced to a use of dehumanization which, instead of numbing them, elicits empathy and pathos for the plight of Mai, Quyen, Truong and all like them who face such dangers in order to flee even worse ones.

Moreover, leaving the reader to dwell on the words "when the sharks attacked" presupposes another attack that will be leveled not only on the fallen body of Truong, but on all "boat people." Here, the sharks are those who would co-opt the image of those fleeing by boat not to create empathy, understanding, and welcoming, but to exclude, reject, and undermine the refugee status of those who have undertaken such a journey.

As we have seen, if "The Boat" were taught alone in the English literature classroom, it would indeed begin a process of breaking down statistical numbing and rhetorical constructions. Yet, this process can also be augmented through the addition of graphical and interactive elements seen in the online adaptation of "The Boat."

Graphic Representations: Augmenting Affect

The power of graphic narratives to create in their readers a sense of empathy for an experience outside of their own has been outlined by numerous scholars. Sarah Birge has observed how what she calls comics' "unique narrative geometries" allow for a representation of so-called "invisible" disabilities, such as autism, in a way such that those not experiencing such shifts in their own perception of the world can better appreciate an experience outside of their own. Specifically, Birge finds that "The specifics of the form allow for a range of representations of specific features of autism: for example, the overwhelming chaos of intensified or unfiltered sensory inputs can be displayed with glaring colors, overlapping borders, and jagged lines," concluding that, "comics provide a means by which to see into another's life, and therein recognize our own" (Birge). Where Birge is talking about the representation of the "other" in terms of disability, the same applies to the representation of refugees taking the perilous boat journey to Australia as seen in the adaptation of "The Boat."

Similar to Birge, Suzanne Keen has analyzed the use of anthropomorphism in comic books to engender empathy. Of particular note in her study is the use of the technique to break down walls of hostility and preconception when it comes to the ethnic Other in situations of conflict. Keen calls the use of such anthropomorphism "ambassadorial strategic empathy," a technique used to "reach readers outside the boundaries of the depicted social world in an effort to change attitudes and even solicit assistance in the real world" (135). While *The Boat* does not use anthropomorphism, it does cover subject matter similar to that analyzed by Keen and, as we will see, a similar process of empathy is produced.

This is not the first time graphic representations have been used to depict the experience of the "Other" in Australian society. A similar process takes place in Shaun Tan's 2007 book *The Arrival*. This book, made up entirely of wordless images, depicts the struggle of a man who has arrived in a country not his own. The lack of recognizable language in the text puts the reader in the place of someone who finds themselves somewhere with no knowledge of language, customs, and expectations. Empathy is created as the reader walks through the text in the "Other's" shoes. One study found that when this text was taught in a classroom made up of students from non-migrant backgrounds, the effect demonstrated that students began to understand and empathize with the difficulties of an "arrival" such as the one depicted in the text (Farrell, Arizpe, and McAdam).

Tan also used a similar technique of empathy creation in his role as illustrator of the book *The Rabbits* (with John Marsden in 2000). However, instead of depicting the experience from the point of view of a new arrival in another culture, this story is an allegorical retelling of the European takeover of Australia, as told from the point of view of Indigenous Australians. Here, it is the original inhabitants for whom empathy is engendered, through casting the European arrival in terms of a plague of rabbits, irrevocably altering the land and landscape. Reflecting on all of his work, Tan sees the aims of his unique art style as "using empathy to get through, overcoming apathy" (Pauli). This process is also achieved through the adaptation of "The Boat."

The graphic adaptation of "The Boat" by Matt Huynh is another text which uses images to communicate the experience of the "Other" in Australian society. The website is designed to draw the reader into the experience of those onboard the boat. As the images and sound initially download, the reader is prompted to insert headphones, which has the effect of blocking out all external noises and drawing the reader into the world of the text. The opening screen shows falling rain and a small fishing boat being tossed in the waves. The boat is shown at mid distance, large enough so that the details of the vessel are evident to the reader, but small enough that its precarious position in the large battering waves is clear. This image establishes not only the size of the boat, into which the reader will soon see have been crammed hundreds of desperate people, attempting to flee from peril, but demonstrates the greater peril they have placed themselves in, and the mercy they find themselves at as the wind, rain, and waves descend upon the boat. The stark black and white color palate of the opening screen, and indeed most of the text itself, underscores the stark realities represented in the text. Thus the scene is set, and the titular boat is firmly established in the reader's mind.

As the reader scrolls down the screen, the opening image of the boat is replaced with text taken from Le's story, as well as accompanying images. Like the boat itself, these images are tossed and turned by the waves, coming in at odd angles and moving in time with the boat as it crashes up and down against the waves. The dark background shows the storm that rages. Augmenting the words are flashes of lightning which pepper across the screen at unpredictable intervals. These oddly timed appearances make the already evocative textual descriptions more tangible. More than just imagining the wind that "screamed," limbs that are "panicked," and people who are "clawing" for direction, the audioscape communicates the experience so the reader is placed in the same position as the characters, the jolting movement of the text evoking the tumble of bodies, and the flashes of lightning evoking the very rage of the storm the characters are so fearful of.

With the boat and the storm established, the first image of those onboard the boat is shown. At first, all the reader can see is a jumble of bodies crashing together in the hull of the boat. Very few faces are shown, only disembodied hands, arms, legs, and feet. This has several effects. First, the sheer mass of people is depicted: the bodies are countless in their shapelessness. Yet, despite the lack of distinction in most of the bodies, a few faces appear here and there. If these faces did not appear, the text would run the risk of further adding to the dehumanizing of the refugee experience by Australian political and media representations. As it is, the few faces in the crowd show the individual humanity amidst the mass of turmoil, and their faces show their fear.

The first character shown in complete detail is Truong, the small boy around whom the whole narrative is centered. In contrast to the mass of humanity pictured above, he is shown alone. In contrast to the facelessness of the crowd, his face is clearly depicted, center frame, completely and almost unearthly bright-white. His white face, described by text above it as "ceramic," glows brightly against the grey background. The outline of his eyes, nose, and lips are evoked in minimal detail, allowing his face to take the focus away from another key detail, his arms encircling his small body, as if holding himself together. The clarity of his face as it is first depicted is contrasted with a later montage where his face appears almost countless times, over and over, with varying degrees of clarity, some full features, some almost disfigured, some disappearing like mist. The change in his appearance is tied to the words accompanying it: "It was his face" is separated, standing out to the right of the image. And below, there is an explanation of what it is about his face that troubles Mai; that he has the same look her father did after the trauma he faced at the re-education camps. Another image of Truong appears later. In contrast to the first, where he is white against the black background of the ship, here he is surrounded by all white. Where much of the first image was a large, clear representation of his face, here his whole body is shown. The reason for this is clear: he is small, malnourished, close to death. The clear "ceramic" nature of his face is gone; instead it is twisted, almost inhuman in appearance. The journey, as well as his sickness, has changed him. This is a visual representation of what the written text does so well—using the technique of dehumanization to empathic effect.

In three images, Truong's narrative journey is shown to parallel the journey of the boat itself. Truong first flees a situation of great trauma, only to have the trauma not only follow him, but take its toll, twisting and deforming the "ceramic," impassive child into a small, pained figure near death. Where Truong's death is the climactic moment both of the story and the adaptation, the graphic format allows for a powerful foreshadowing of his fate. Earlier in the text, a body is shown being thrown into the water in a series of images descending down the page. This is later echoed when Mai and Quyen surrender Truong to the same fate, the image of his small body also shown descending into the depths of the ocean, never to see land. The visual narrative of Truong's journey on the boat reveals not only the trauma of such journeys, but the real and palpable peril faced by those who take such journeys.

Several times, the reader is able to leave the boat while the narrative takes a break from the current events of the timeline to give details of those that led to the journey Mai is taking. It is here that the sounds of the boat, the crashing waves, the bodies jumbling against one another, and the telltale heaving of humans vomiting are replaced, and the reader is given a reprieve. In the stories from Mai's past, there is a quiet calm as images appear of Mai and her parents, accompanied not by the violent waves in the boat sections, but instead red flowers of her homeland—the only color used in the entire text. But soon the flowers disappear and the reason for Mai's boat journey is made clear. Her father is shown, haunted and skeletal, wounds evident on his body from tortures he has endured. Their lives are in danger, and the only safe option for Mai is to escape.

Where the link between the textual world and the real world is implied in the short story, and evoked by knowledge of Nam Le's own similar journey to Australia, the visual medium is able to make such a link overt. At times, the hand-drawn narrative is interspersed with photographic images. These have the effect of reminding the reader that, while the story is a fictionalized account, it is based on real events people experienced coming to Australia, people such as the author Nam Le himself. The reader's journey ends with a photograph of men, women, and children looking over the stern of a boat not unlike the one depicted in the story. Not only does the image bring home the reality behind the story just read, but is also accompanied by some historical facts about the experience of Vietnamese refugees who fled to Australia.

This closing image poses a question: Which is more effective in producing the form of affect described by Slovic? Is it the story, the hand-drawn images, the photograph, or the statistics? Perhaps it is by using all four in concert that this text is able to circumvent the attention-splitting effect seen in the study performed by Small, Slovic, and Lowenstein. Ideally, we can use texts like "The Boat" in our classrooms to engender empathy in our students, facilitating the victim-identifiability effect to overcome statistical numbness and compassion fatigue, as well as to reclaim and rewrite misleading political discourses.

I am not alone in claiming that graphic representations such as "The Boat" can be used to engender empathy in student understanding of the Other. Megan Boler argued for a similar yet more nuanced approach through her teaching of the graphic novel *Maus* by Art Spiegelman, a depiction of life under the regime of Nazi Germany. Beyond mere "passive empathy," as Boler calls it, where students are simply presented with a text designed to create emotion, or, empathy as consumption, Boler believes that in order for students to truly imagine the horrors of the Holocaust from reading *Maus*, they must instead read stories and statistics "until it becomes, precisely, *un*imaginable" (261, emphasis original). Boler's study was published in 1997 and, as I have shown, in the internet age, such reading of stories and statistics and *unimaginability* have already taken place for many students before being presented with the text. As such, this process is unnecessary in today's classrooms. Instead, I believe that empathetic reading of graphic texts is an antidote to much of the apathetic malaise of mass knowledge consumption.

Conclusion

Literature has the power to produce empathy in readers. Empathy is an essential step to break through issues in communication, such as statistical numbing and scope severity paradox. Graphic novels can greatly increase the process of empathy by highlighting the visual sense and drawing the reader further into the experience of the "Other." Interactive graphic novels have even greater power, as the user engages by reading, listening, and propelling themselves through the narrative; even with something as simple as the roll of a mouse wheel, this act has the power to create a greater emotional link between the reader and the subject matter.

Empathy created through the immersive nature of the online comic could have the effect of breaking through cultural baggage and allowing greater understanding of the personal stories. In light of the recent statistical numbing seen in Australia, where mass data of horrific treatment of asylum seekers was released, only to have public outrage evaporate within days, maybe there is hope through this form. If the experience of adults (and, more tragically, children) in offshore detention in Australia was communicated through story and image, perhaps the horrors of what the Nauru papers revealed, and the horrors of the personal stories of displacement, might be communicated to their true empathic effect. Perhaps, then, real change can take place—if not in the political sphere, certainly in the hearts and minds of our students. What I propose is not a complete solution to statistical blindness in our conception of large-scale suffering such as the Global Refugee Crisis, but it is a step in the right direction.

NOTES

1. This study found that this effect was limited to the consumption of narrative fiction: "Consistent with this idea, our group has shown that frequent readers of narrative fiction perform better on two different empathy tasks, whereas frequent readers of expository non-fiction perform worse." Another study took this distinction further, showing that empathy increased when readers consumed "writerly" (i.e., literary or challenging) texts as opposed to "readerly" (i.e., less challenging and more simplistic) texts (Kidd and Costano 2013; see also Keen 2007).
2. Kurdi's name was initially reported as Aylan in the Western press.
3. The 2014 figure was down from 300 boats with 20,587 people in 2013 and 378 boats with 17,204 people in 2013. The Abbott government would argue that this proved their policies were much more effective in "stopping the boats" than the policies of the previous Rudd/Gillard governments.
4. There is no law in Australia prohibiting the act of arriving in Australia for the purposes of seeking asylum without a valid visa, despite the government's claims to the contrary. And while it is correct that the Australian Migration Act 1958 makes a distinction between "lawful" and "unlawful" non-citizens, it is also true that, by being a signatory to the UN Refugee Convention, the Australian government agrees not to treat asylum seekers as if they have committed an illegal act by seeking asylum in Australia (see "Scott Morrison").
5. The origins and attribution of this quote to Stalin are in some doubt. The *Quote Investigator* website cites an article by Leonard Lyons from the *Washington Post* in 1947 attributing it to Stalin, although it is possible it was not originally said by Stalin, but rather made up by the journalist himself.

Works Cited

"A Single Death is a Tragedy; a Million Deaths is a Statistic." *Quote Investigator*, 2017, http://quoteinvestigator.com/2010/05/21/death-statistic/

Alizadeh, Ali. *Transactions*. Queensland UP, 2013.

Beneba Clarke, Maxine. *Foreign Soil*. Simon & Schuster, 2014.

Boler, Megan. "The Risks of Empathy: Interrogating Multiculturalism's Gaze." *Cultural Studies*, vol. 11, no. 2, 1997, pp. 253–273.

Birge, Sarah. "No Life Lessons Here: Comics, Autism, and Empathetic Scholarship." *Disability Studies Quarterly*, vol.20, no.1, 2010, http://dsq-sds.org/article/view/1067/1255

Costello, Tim. "The road to compassion for the refugees of Syria is paved with good intentions." *The Sydney Morning Herald*, 1 Sept. 2016, http://www.smh.com.au/comment/road-to-compassion-for-the-refugees-of-syria-is-paved-with-good-intentions-20160901-gr6d6j.html

Delingpole, James. "Why should we listen to Benedict Cumberbatch on Syrian refugees?" *The Spectator*, 7 Nov. 2015, http://www.spectator.co.uk/2015/11/why-should-we-listen-to-benedict-cumberbatch-on-syrian-refugees/

Elgot, Jessica. "Father of drowned boy Aylan Kurdi plans to return to Syria." *The Guardian*, 3 Sep. 2015, https://www.theguardian.com/world/2015/sep/03/father-drowned-boy-aylan-kurdi-return-syria

Farrell, Paul, Nick Evershed, and Helen Davidson. "The Nauru files: cache of 2,000 leaked reports reveal scale of abuse of children in Australian offshore detention." *The Guardian*, 10 Aug. 2016, https://www.theguardian.com/australia-news/2016/aug/10/the-nauru-files-2000-leaked-reports-reveal-scale-of-abuse-of-children-in-australian-offshore-detention

Farrell, Maureen, Evelyn Arizpe, and Julie McAdam. "Journeys across Visual Borders: Annotated Spreads of 'The Arrival' by Shaun Tan as a Method for Understanding Pupils' Creation of Meaning through Visual Images." *The Australian Journal of Language and Literacy*, vol.33, no. 3, Oct 2010, pp. 198–210.

George, Sandy. "The sound and vision of The Boat." *Sbs.com.au*, 23 Sep. 2015, http://www.sbs.com.au/movies/article/2015/04/27/sound-and-vision-boat

International Rescue Committee, 2016, https://www.rescue.org/

"Internet Stats & Facts for 2016." HostingFacts, 2017, https://hostingfacts.com/internet-facts-stats-2016/

Johnson, Dan R., Brandie L. Huffman, and Danny M. Jasper. "Changing Race Boundary Perception by Reading Narrative Fiction." *Basic And Applied Social Psychology*, vol. 36, no. 1, 2014, pp. 83–90.

Keen, Suzanne. *Empathy and the Novel*. Oxford UP, 2007.

———. "Fast Tracks to Narrative Empathy: Anthropomorphism and Dehumanization in Graphic Narratives." *SubStance*, vol. 40, no. 1, 2011, pp. 135–155.

Kidd, David Comer, and Emanuele Castano. "Reading Literary Fiction Improves Theory of Mind." *Science*, vol 342, no. 6156, 3 Oct. 2013, pp. 377–380.

Konrath, Sara, Edward O'Brien, and Courtney Hsing. "Changes in Dispositional Empathy in American College Students Over Time: A Meta-Analysis." *Psychology Review*, vol. 15, no. 2, 2011, pp. 180–198.

Le, Nam and Hyunh, Matt (illus). *The Boat*. www.sbs.com.au/theboat

Le, Nam and Hyunh, Matt (illus). *The Boat*.

McMah, Lauren. "PM says border security is paramount despite calls to let asylum seekers stay." *News.com.au*, 7 Feb. 2016, http://www.news.com.au/national/politics/pm-says-border-security-is-paramount-despite-calls-to-let-asylum-seeke rs-stay/news-story/e99e565792833483fce63d051d15737d

Mar, Raymond A, Keith Oatley, Jacob Hirsh, Jennifer dela Paz, and Jordan B Peterson. "Bookworms versus nerds: Exposure to fiction versus non-fiction, divergent associations with social ability, and the simulation of fictional social worlds." *Journal of Research in Personality*, vol. 40, 2006, pp. 694–712.

Marsden, John. Tan, Shaun (illus). *The Rabbits*. Hodder, 2000.

Neumann, Klaus. "'Queue jumpers' and 'boat people': the way we talk about refugees began in 1977." *The Guardian*, 5 Jun. 2015, https://www.thegua rdian.com/commentisfree/2015/jun/05/queue-jumpers-and-boat-people-the-way-we-talk-about-refugees-began-in-1977

Nordgren, Loran F. and Mary-Hunter Morris McDonnell. "The Scope-Severity Paradox: Why Doing More Harm Is Judged to Be Less Harmful." *Social Psychological and Personality Science*, vol. 2, no. 1, 2011, pp. 97–102.

Pauli, Michelle. "Shaun Tan's Unexpected Details." *The Guardian*, 27 Jul. 2009, https://www.theguardian.com/books/2009/jul/27/shaun-tan-unexpected-de tails

Phillips, Janet. "Boat arrivals and boat 'turnbacks' in Australia since 1976: a quick guide to the statistics." *Parliament of Australia*, 11 Sep. 2015, http://www.aph. gov.au/About_Parliament/Parliamentary_Departments/Parliamentary_Library/pubs/rp/rp1516/Quick_Guides/BoatTurnbacks

"Scott Morrison correct on 'illegal entry' of people without a visa." *FactCheck*, 13 Sep. 2013, http://www.abc.net.au/news/2013-09-06/morrison-correct-ille gal-entry-people/4935372

Slovic, Paul. "Psychic Numbing and Genocide." *American Psychological Association*, Nov. 2007, http://www.apa.org/science/about/psa/2007/11/slovic.aspx

Small, Deborah A., Paul Slovic, and George Lowenstein. "Sympathy and callousness: The impact of deliberative thought on donations to identifiable and statistical victims." *Organizational Behavior and Human Decision Processes*, vol. 102, no. 2, Mar 2007, pp. 143–153.

Tickner, Robert. "There's no legal queue. And three other facts Australians get wrong about asylum seekers." *The Guardian,* 15 Jun. 2015, https://www.theg uardian.com/commentisfree/2015/jun/15/theres-no-legal-queue-and-three-other-facts-australians-get-wrong-about-asylum-seekers

United Nations High Commissioner for Refugees. "Figures at a Glance." UNHCR, 2016a, http://www.unhcr.org/en-us/figures-at-a-glance.html

———. "Syria Fact Sheet." 2016b, http://reporting.unhcr.org/sites/default/files/UNHCR%20Syria%20Fact%20Sheet%20-%20November%202016.pdf

Zac, Paul. "How Stories Change the Brain." *The Greater Good,* 17 Dec. 2013, http://greatergood.berkeley.edu/article/item/how_stories_change_brain

Zarracina, Javier. "The stunning scope of the world's refugee crisis, in charts." *Vox.com* 30 Dec. 2015, http://www.vox.com/2015/12/30/10684672/in-2015-one-of-122-persons-worldwide-was-a-refugee

Performative Texts and the Pedagogical Theatre: Alison Bechdel's *Fun Home* as Compositional Model

William Cordeiro and Season Ellison

Alison Bechdel's text *Fun Home: A Family Tragicomic* is a rich, multimodal text we have incorporated into many of our freshman- and sophomore-level Honors composition and general education first-year seminar classes. Depending on the course and audience, we have approached *Fun Home* from a number of angles: generically in relation to the Bildungsroman, as a memoir, as a Gothic novel, as a graphic novel, and, more specifically, as a model of performativity[1] embedded by and within the text as well as within the writing process. Regardless of our varied approaches to teaching the text, we recognize that *Fun Home* both performs and is about identity performance; it prompts students and instructors alike to recognize the performed identities of the readers, characters, text, and author.

A strength of Bechdel's novel is her complex and performative layering of alphabetic text, images, and spatial relationships, as well as her inclusion and layering of familial and canonical resources. Each layer adds complexity to the graphic memoir and it quickly becomes clear that a reader must, like

W. Cordeiro (✉)
Northern Arizona University, Flagstaff, AZ, USA

S. Ellison
Bemidji State University, Bemidji, MN, USA

© The Author(s) 2018
A. Burger (ed.), *Teaching Graphic Novels in the English Classroom*,
DOI 10.1007/978-3-319-63459-3_11

Alison,[2] develop diverse skills to "read" these textual layerings well. Many traditionally aged, starting college students focus mostly on alphabetic words to discern the meaning of a given text; however, learning to recognize reading as an active performance that requires shared participation can help students envision a fuller picture of reading as an iterative process. To grasp an overall understanding of *Fun Home*, it is necessary to examine the interrelations between alphabetic text, images, and spatial layout, as well as the gaps or differences between these modalities that often reveal discrepant, ambiguous, or ironic meanings.

Bechdel's memoir illustrates how graphic novels can represent the process of identity formation and the recognitions needed to understand how our identities are, largely, created or performed. Alongside deconstructing seemingly private and publicly performed identities, *Fun Home* brings to the fore the reciprocal conventions and iterative rehearsals that shape one's social roles and sense of self. Perhaps the performative process of identity formation, as represented in the novel, is summed up best by a brief analysis of the cover image of the 2006 edition of *Fun Home*. This image displays, at once, a drawing of a silver-tinted photograph of a young Alison looking wistfully at the reader, who views her father in profile. The image serves as a distorted mirror, wherein the audience member's face is literally laid over those of Alison and her father in a palimpsest of reflective gazes. Each layer alters the signification of another. Similarly, the title's echo of a "fun house" hints at the varied connotations of this particular combination of words: a fun home, used ironically given that Alison does not recognize her childhood home as "fun"; a funhouse, which represents the distorted qualities of identity formation and familial narratives; and, more practically, as a shortened version of the words "funeral home," which is where Alison's father works until his untimely death. We experience these textual meanings, alongside the drawn graphic of Alison and her father, the literal feel of the slick and shiny cover, and, if we read carefully, Bechdel's embedded hint toward identity formation (as seeing oneself simultaneously projected onto the characters depicted distorts both characters and reader).

Bechdel's novel encourages close, intertextual, feminist, and queer readings. The texts and images contained within the pages of *Fun Home* mirror[3] the identity discoveries made by the characters and hint at the potential identity discoveries (whether familial, gendered, sexual, or intellectual) our students may experience. These layers of identity make the text particularly applicable to our early-career students as they are learning to develop and negotiate their beliefs beyond those they have institutionalized throughout their childhood and adolescence. These negotiations can be scary, and many students identify with Alison's struggles, whether or not they are able to identify with her sexual orientation. It is rare for one of us to have students in a class who have not hidden parts of their identities from other people for fear of being dismissed or, even worse, punished.

As we engage with students in deeper analyses of these relationships between performing the text in our classrooms and the characters' performative discoveries throughout the narrative, students develop new understandings of how performance as a concept—including the performance of composition—can support their ideas. They realize that composition extends well beyond the words and sentence structures they use to convey a claim; composition is an ongoing and performative process that is part of their lived realities. The students who reach this understanding see how their compositional voices should reflect the subject matters they discuss. Thus, many students begin to see writing as a creative and exploratory process, which moves them beyond their preconceived notions of academic scholarship. In fact, these varied approaches to reading and generating texts, applied more broadly, demonstrate the pivotal role the humanities play in eliciting curiosity, social understanding, and personal growth.

In this chapter, we investigate *Fun Home* as an artifact framed using our pedagogic performances across differently focused composition and seminar-based courses. We put forward the concept of "pedagogical theatre" to illustrate how strong pedagogy should be fluid, flexible, shifting, nebulous, and always in rehearsal. Like the characters in Bechdel's graphic memoir, we continually negotiate our relationships with students, our relationships with texts, and our relationships with writing. We co-write in a unified and collaborative voice to reinforce our claim that strong pedagogy is also collaborative, that strong scholarship is an exploratory process, and that strong writing should reflect the content contained within.

The Pedagogical Theatre

Generally speaking, our classrooms are most often the sites of pedagogical theatre. As Bryant Alexander argues in the introduction to *Performance Theories in Education: Power, Pedagogy, and the Politics of Identity*, "the classroom, with teachers and students engaged in the processes of education establishes culture" (ch. 1). Cultivating this culture is central to developing a successful pedagogical theatre space in which learners feel safe to explore, act, and rehearse paradigm-shifting performances of identity, which might include a new-found identity as a writer. In essence, the classroom "becomes a practiced place; a site in which diverse beings come together in order to engage and negotiate knowledge, systems of understanding, and ways of being, seeing, knowing, and doing" (ibid.). Thus, performance studies-based pedagogy incorporates active learning methods and is self-reflexive.

Beyond a literal classroom performance space, we also propose that a pedagogical theatre can serve as a conceptual framework to help us consider teaching as iterative, interactive, and ever-adaptive. In this section, we examine how our own and our students' roles in this classroom theatre stem from both individually contextualized and socially scripted behaviors. We explore the ongoing and reciprocally evolving relationships *between* the performance of the instructors and the performance of the students' identities within this classroom performance space—and we suggest that no single actor can function without influencing another. Finally, it is important to note that a pedagogical theatre is enhanced when we study a text, such as *Fun Home*, that embraces and models performativity.

Richard Schechner's notion of "restored behavior" is one avenue through which performance studies scholars conceptualize "performance" beyond formal artistic practice and into a broader social context. In the 1960s, Schechner articulated that:

> Restored behavior is symbolic and reflexive: not empty but loaded behavior multivocally broadcasting significances. These difficult terms express a single principle: The self can act in/as another; the social or transindividual self is a role or set of roles. Symbolic and reflexive behavior is the hardening into theater of social, religious, aesthetic, medical, and educational processes. (36)

The repertoire, or store, of symbolic gestures and codes of various social roles is repeated and rehearsed until the self is embodied, shaped, and "hardened" into a more definite sense that is increasingly apparent to others and instinctive for the actor. Goals of what we deem "pedagogical theatre," then, are to recognize these institutions and behaviors as "hardening" processes, to analyze how these processes come to exist, and to question why people participate in them.

The second portion of Schechner's definition extends these ideas. He writes: "Performance means: never for the first time. It means: for the second to the *n*th time. Performance is 'twice-behaved behavior' and 'is always subject to revision'" (Schechner 36–37). Institutions and identities alike are created by a process of repeating behavior. Any particular behavior may be encouraged or dissuaded, depending on an institution's goals. In a pedagogical theatre, we deconstruct the social and internal pressures that encourage or dissuade particular (and already rehearsed) behaviors. We hope that the use of performance as a conceptual paradigm helps students to better understand how our world is made of symbolic and systemically rehearsed behaviors, as deemed appropriate by the institutions in which we all participate. It is through our own performative pedagogical philosophies that we model these complex processes for our students. In fact, it is common for performance studies-influenced educators to see both teaching and reading as performative acts, if not performative arts. How the concept of performativity might influence or even enhance the pedagogical practices of instructors from other disciplines has been explored far less often.

From this particular interdisciplinary perspective, our teaching of *Fun Home* highlights how different performance modalities mutually mirror, distort, and shape each other. The concept of performativity might help students and instructors become comfortable with and curious about such interrelationships and ambiguity. Discussing restored behavior can help students to better understand the layers of multivalent pressures on both individuals and groups to embody or portray an identity in a particular manner. In class we often invoke performance concepts as means to cultivate deeper critical, creative, and reflexive thinking about reading.

In the graphic novel, Alison experiences a transformative coming-of-age in which she not only learns new critical and affective approaches to reading, but also negotiates new relationships with a series of teachers and mentor figures. Her education is informed by her overbearing father (who also happens to be her English teacher), her somewhat distant mother (who is, in fact, an actor), as well as a college professor, her grandmother, siblings, fellow students, and various friends and lovers. In addition, Alison's newly forming self-understanding is influenced by a series of feminist, queer, existential, and literary writers alongside the fictional characters and theoretical ideas she encounters as she devours copious resources to form her personal canon. In fact, a major facet of Alison's growth in the novel stems from her learning how to read complex literature and images. She then expands on her learning and applies these new skills to interpret her past, the performative constructions of gender and sexuality, and human motivations and desires. Each of these applications opens up spaces that demonstrate how one kind of reading may sometimes be discrepant or disparate with another kind of reading.

Throughout the memoir, Alison's iterative performance of reading is visualized through highlights, cross-outs, doodles, marginal notes, and other marks, including, at one point, smears of her blood. These various marks construct a "scriptable" text in which the reader's rehearsal of codes and meanings actively remakes new significations, often in a messy and tentative way. Furthermore, such marks provide students with models to engage with texts by inscribing their own interpretations and remarks onto them in an ongoing and consciously constructive process of close reading. This process is social and individual; Alison's mentors and teachers help her discover new approaches to reading, in some cases by inscribing their comments on her writing. From this palimpsest, Alison forms a more holistic sense of self. As a character, she constructs and rehearses her identity and, as an author, she creates and revises her journal, letters, school papers, and ultimately the graphic memoir itself.

Shared mimetic performances, between classroom actors and textual acting, extend the performativity embedded in *Fun Home* beyond the graphic memoir and into the realm of lived realities and socially rehearsed behaviors. In doing so, the performance context has the potential to produce a self-critical, meta-cognitive, multimodal collaboration between teachers and students, among students, and between readers and text. In our own case, we extend this mimetic collaboration and the concept of a pedagogical theatre to our shared relationship as educators. But, perhaps most importantly, given that we teach composition, we hope students learn to see that a successful writing process, like an effective rehearsal process and an effective learning process, is rarely "finished" but remains shifting, fluid, and provisional.

Thus, in a composition classroom, a pedagogical theatre occurs where and when a written text:

- is reflexive of teaching and learning activities;
- generates mutually influential relationships between the performance of the text and the performance of the readers;
- encourages students to critique "hardened" identities or institutions as constructions and consider the underlying performative processes that create the identity or institution in question;
- illustrates how identity formation is rehearsed;
- emphasizes the use-value of process over product, especially in learning and composition.

Conceiving of writing as a "rehearsal process" helps students see that writing means more than words on a page, arranged into sentences, or paragraphs, or even chapters. In fact, if we maintain that writing is rehearsed, then we should consider some of the experiences we create to help students negotiate this rehearsal process.

COMPOSITION IN PRACTICE

In our pedagogical theatres we focus largely on "doing" or, to use theatre terminology, "action." Composition instructor Jason Todd argues that "we don't learn by listening, but by doing. Content delivery is only one component of effective teaching, and despite what most of us learned in school, it is not the most important" (11). Todd bases his argument on Bill Tucker's observations about flipped classrooms in *Education Next*: "instruction that used to occur in class is now accessed at home, in advance of class. Class becomes the place to work through problems, advance concepts and engage in collaborative learning" (82). As Todd summarizes, "in short, the classroom becomes a place for active and engaged learning" and he posits that graphic novels are excellent resources to help students learn in active ways.

To foster action, to help students "work through" the "problems" of reading a challenging text such as *Fun Home*, and to integrate the social skills we learn together in our collective lives, we employ a variety of traditional and non-traditional educational approaches. Our class activities might include visual, spatial, somatic, or collaborative explorations. In this section, we detail select activities that have illuminated our study of *Fun Home*. Additionally, these practical exercises largely enhance and embrace the concept of pedagogical theatre by honing our attention to reflect on the conscious and unconscious performances present in the narrative and behavioral texts. Such reflection goes a long way toward engendering understandings that extend beyond the walls of the classroom, which demonstrates that pedagogical theatre can potentially exist anywhere.

Visual

One of the most powerful ways to help students develop proficiency in visual reading strategies is to design lessons that ensure they must rely on visual rather than verbal media to convey their ideas. Many of these techniques could be described as "boardwork," wherein students—sometimes after preliminary discussion in small groups or pairs—write or draw their responses to a prompt on the board using different techniques, such as concept mapping, theme webs, or collaging.[4] Collaging involves students writing and drawing fragments, quotes, and/or doodles on the board as a form of brainstorming; later, the collage can act as a springboard for discussion as the students elaborate more in-depth responses prompted by others' collaged elements.

To push students to learn how to articulate their ideas beyond words alone, we have also used artistic collage and other visual and creative media. We might provide a prompt, such as: "Create an artistic initial response to your first reading of *Fun Home*." The students are provided with art materials: paper, crayons, pencils, markers, tape, wood, glue, paint, pipe cleaners, images, and a host of other tactile and visual tools. Using only these materials and no words, the students create a visual response to represent their initial reaction to the text, which may be abstract or realistic. Because students are generally more confident using verbal or written communication to convey their ideas, asking them to use artistic and creative means of communicating may feel uncomfortable to them. Oftentimes, students worry that they are "not artists"; however, because a variety of materials are provided, they need not rely on their drawing skills alone. Collages of images and other material objects are common products of this exercise and, upon completion of their artwork, they switch with a classmate. They then interpret their partners' projects, with no input from the partners, before the original artists can clarify their intended interpretations. In so doing, students learn how visual representation is integral to making sense of our daily lives and why it must thus be carefully read. In fact, the fullest understandings can only be reached by conducting multiple readings, no matter how simple the initial representation seems to be. This exercise encourages students to consider why deconstructing the complex visual representations of *Fun Home* is significant in developing a clearer understanding of the graphic text.

Projecting and annotating a single panel is yet another visual technique that encourages students to see how, like this artistic project, one element from a graphic novel might evoke multiple interpretations—some potentially conflicting. Students may underline, circle, and point out small details, whether these are aspects of the alphabetic text, the graphic figures, the spatial layout, or the relationships between these layered elements. The students then write brief notes about their chosen feature(s), which forces them to focus on the granular level of textual analysis that close, critical reading requires. Often, the most revealing moments of this exercise occur when students choose to annotate the same feature of the text, but their annotations divulge different possibilities of meaning. Thus, students are faced with a visual representation of divergent interpretations, which encourages them to embrace that reading is not a univocal performance. With more advanced students or with repeated training, modeling, and rehearsal, this activity can be codified by requiring that each student (or group of students) annotates multiple meanings for different features of the text. When students can articulate disparate interpretations, they can more consciously discuss and better evaluate the merits of those interpretations; this skill is often one of the most difficult but rewarding to teach and one that employing graphic novels as a learning tool can facilitate with uncommon ease.

Spatial

Assuming emphasis is given specifically to the arrangement, layout, and relationship between figures, panels, and spacing (and that an exercise incorporates analysis of how these elements relate to each other and to time), spatial exercises like storyboarding and graphic writing often go beyond merely representing visual modalities and can be useful in helping students decode complex spatial arrangements. Hillary Chute notes, "A comics page offers a rich temporal map configured as much by what isn't drawn as by what is: it is highly conscious of the artificiality of its selective borders, which diagram the page into an arrangement of encapsulated moments" (455). Beyond making temporal connections, spatial relationships also often convey important information regarding the figures' emotions and experiences, and the characters' perspectives about the events depicted. All of these elements are encoded in subtle ways that many students initially need help to parse.

Introducing students to a basic vocabulary used to interpret graphic novels—such as gutter, frame, bleed, panel, and graphic weight—aids students' growing perceptions of spatial design and the meanings such design might convey. This vocabulary can be supplemented with vocabulary adopted from visual arts, cinema, or theatre. When students have a basic grasp of potential terms they might use to identify spatial features and the temporal or emotional cues these terms invoke, students are more likely to pick up on these cues and appreciate their significance as they read.

We have both employed *Fun Home* as a model to assist students to think spatially. One potential exercise is to have students create a storyboard to represent a revelatory moment from their own lives, such as Alison's textual realization that she is, in fact, lesbian (Bechdel 74). As one might in film, students create a frame-by-frame outline of their own experience, mostly using visual imagery, to convey the basic arc of their story. From the storyboard, students might create a graphic representation, adding alphabetic text into the mix and revising the initial storyboard to ensure the visual and textual imagery work as a unit to convey their intended meaning and illustrate the passage of time. In fact, when students create their own graphic texts, the sophistication of their composition skills often increases because they learn to coordinate and layer spatial and temporal cues into their visual and verbal stories.

Somatic

In conjunction with teaching *Fun Home* alongside other texts written about sexuality and gender,[5] we have assigned similar projects that prompt self-reflection and critical thought about systemic social norms and the performative processes that constitute these normative institutions. In short, we ask students to engage in activities that encourage them to feel as if their routine gender comportment, identity, or expression is altered in some manner, or we ask them to imagine an empathetic response to another person's identity performance and act "as if" they experience that identity for a specified amount of time. Such activities could include engaging in various types of cross-dressing, physical activities (say, a dance class or a pick-up football game), acting in ways that are less typical of the student's self-defined gendered norms, or walking from the classroom to the bookstore and back imagining the potential experience "as if"[6] one identified as genderqueer, differently abled, or visibly non-white. The choice to complete a preferred activity is an important component necessary to provide agency to students as they explore.

Such assignments do not depend on a conventional binary system, since one's self-defined identifications are specified in terms of each student's habitual patterns, behaviors, norms, and performances. We want students to experiment with performing identities beyond their own in an attempt to understand Alison and her father's experiences, as well as the lived experiences of people who populate our students' lives. We also want our students to feel relatively safe in doing so. As students tackle these often ideologically challenging assignments, they should not put themselves or others into situations in which they would be unduly stressed or feel danger; should students fear they might experience significant discomfort, a viable option is to provide an alternative assignment in advance.

Students first describe the gender norms[7] to which they already subscribe in an effort to better understand their initial gender performance and establish a baseline for the activity. Next, they define the social contexts and norms that drive their chosen activity. They are coached to consider how the gender-performance activity pushes them to reflect on their own sense of identity by clearly articulating the performative choices related to gender expression and physical comportment that they make as they complete the exercise. When carefully guided, many students are able to recognize that their behavioral choices frequently reflect and reinforce a binary way of thinking about gender. Because students approach the activity as participant-observers and are encouraged to reflect deeply about the understandings the activity generates, they can often see how their actions and reactions are influenced by surrounding institutional contexts and cultural ideals. Furthermore, they sometimes discern how, through their choices, they unintentionally participate in the further hardening of processes that create problematic social institutions and practices. Perhaps more importantly, because during the exercise they imagined what it might be like to live life with an identity different from their own, students often conclude the activity better able to empathize with other people.

Students commonly report that these assignments are revelatory. One self-identified female student who typically wore jeans, sweatshirts, and little or no make-up, for example, was shocked to see how differently her mother treated her when she wore stereotypically feminine dresses and make-up as a part of the assignment. Another student, who experimented with a genderqueer look, discovered that this look was actually their preferred gender expression and, gaining confidence through this prompt, began transitioning to a new-found gender identity. A third student, who explored campus "as if" she identified as a heterosexual white male, saw other people in ways she hadn't considered before. Though she was mostly imagining, she reported that she became more aware of how other seemingly heterosexual white males on campus unknowingly caused reactions in people's behavior as they went about their day. She observed that women or seemingly genderqueer students often gave the young white men more space than they were granted themselves. As we integrate these exercises alongside our study of *Fun Home*, we find that a wide variety of students are consistently inspired by Alison's gender and sexual explorations, which provide them with the impetus to explore different behavioral repertoires, identities, comportments, and expressions when they participate in these activities. Thus, the exercises encourage students to reflect on how gender and other social roles are constructed and performed both internally and externally and how rehearsed behavior is a primary component of these constructions.

Collaborative

Many of the exercises and assignments we've discussed require students to work together. In fact, collaborating is central to theorizing and practicing pedagogical theatre; without actors and audiences there would be no exchange of ideas. Furthermore, pedagogical theatre invites students and instructors to serve in both actor and audience roles. Without purposeful and precise attention to collaboration, the theatrical metaphor that undergirds this chapter would be incomplete; thus, in this section we provide examples of how we engage in collaborative activities with our students.

When students literally act out or stage sections of text, they learn to rehearse a variety of skills such as collaboration, role-playing, filling in temporal gaps, and configuring a three-dimensional space. They must also interpret images, symbols, and alphabetic texts to realize which parts of their understanding of the novel are merely inferred and then discern whether to leave out or include these inferences in performance. In our experience, some students resist the idea of using performance as a medium with which to digest another text because they feel acting puts them on display and exposes them to their peers' scrutiny. One way we have dealt with this fear is to lower the stakes by allowing small groups to rehearse in different rooms and, if they require it, to only perform for the instructor and one another. By contrast, some classes have readily embraced creating theatrical performances and, in these cases, we have sometimes used venues where other students, friends, professors, and staff members act as an audience. Either way, we emphasize the imperfect and provisional nature of the performance and reinforce that even the seeming failures of the students' stagings often illuminate the text and help us to explore our sense of self.

Another collaborative activity that has proven useful is to suggest or require that students co-author papers or engage in collaborative writing assignments. While this practice is commonplace in other fields—especially in the sciences—most humanities courses implicitly emphasize an ethic of solitary endeavor and supposedly meritocratic individualism by enforcing that students write their papers alone. The benefits of co-authoring assignments are manifold. To begin, students have two or more viewpoints on an assigned text, which makes finding multiple or more sophisticated interpretations of it easier. Co-authoring prompts students to more explicitly plan and utilize the various steps of the writing process as well as develop a better awareness of the underlying processes that generate sound research, organization, tone, sentence structure, and argumentation. Furthermore, shared writing assignments help students overcome writer's block by providing a partner with whom they can discuss and share ideas, and incorporate the idea of an authentic audience—the peer collaborator—into the actual writing process, which reinforces the notion of audience as an important tenet of compositional rhetoric. Students learn important skills from each other and will often invest much more effort in peer review when a grade is shared rather than individualized. While it is true that a few students may resent collaborative writing because they fear one student might shirk their responsibilities, there are techniques to ensure accountability. Individual students can write narratives detailing the writing process. Students can choose their own partners. We might scaffold a structure that breaks the paper into smaller, scheduled steps and require check-ins with student groups that start when the assignment prompt is initially given and conclude only when the final paper is due. Indeed, we co-author this chapter because we believe in the many benefits of collaborative authorship and modeling the techniques we ask of our students.

What is challenging about these types of collaborations is that the players must abdicate partial control of the exercise to other participants. This challenge works on two levels: at the level of peer-to-peer, wherein students must learn to trust their peers in order to truly collaborate well; and on the level of instructor-to-student, wherein the instructor must learn to trust the students and let go of total control of the classroom experience. Shared authority, which on the surface is generally celebrated, is also potentially unnerving because it means allowing your work to be influenced by and dependent on other people's ideas and work ethics. Thus, in close collaborations, like those outlined in this section, it is possible that a student's or an instructor's idea might be challenged, but it is equally possible that a challenge, at first perceived as a threat, might also deepen and strengthen one's initial ideas. In fact, many of our best ideas, exercises, and pedagogical successes have stemmed from moments of potential conflict and/or challenges to our own and other students' original proposals.

A Performative Model for Reading

Fun Home is largely *about* performing—and audiencing—myriad intertextual and intersectional types of readings that push students to integrate their academic experiences into their lived experiences. Due to its modeling of such connections, many students find Bechdel's memoir particularly relevant, and in class we often explore these connections using performance theory. For example, the layering of canonical and non-canonical literary and artistic texts in *Fun Home* might be read as performative intertextuality, wherein the inclusion of the conceptual frame "performative" reinforces the meaning-making potential of the intertexts and highlights that these texts are both framed *within* their own contexts and also selected by Bechdel *to* frame a theme that further develops Alison's character. Relatedly, Bechdel highlights intersectionality, which illustrates how one identity performance influences, supports, or even negates another identity performance in a regenerative iteration of identity formation. Performative intertexts and identities are further influenced, enhanced, and/or altered by performative contexts like the walls of the classroom, the parameters of an assignment, the plot of a graphic novel, or the panels of a comic, which frame the performative acts themselves. Thus, the inclusion of performance theory has enhanced our studies of *Fun Home* and prompted students to think creatively about critical analysis of the text and how its meanings might be synthesized from other texts and structures of lived reality. Practically, generating the deep connections required by these highly theoretical concepts teaches students to better connect their thoughts in composition and in class discussions. Finally, a main goal we seek to achieve within our pedagogical theatre is to acknowledge and deconstruct the ways that texts, identities, and contexts interrelate to craft a generative, full-fledged performance that is the lived reality we mutually experience and know.

In the graphic novel, Alison's identity recognitions largely stem from reading and rereading, which prompt her continually expanding awareness of her own and others' performative identities. In one of our interdisciplinary Honors classes, studying *Fun Home* helped students understand theoretical ideas they had read about but previously found difficult to conceptualize. Despite initial struggles, students were surprised to see that, upon rereading, they *could* apply Michel Foucault's theories about power and institutional norms to better understand the pressures and assumptions that shape Alison's emerging intersectional identity. The idea that overlapping, competing social norms—whether bureaucratic or familial—exert mutually informing pressures on one's expression of self, sexuality, and gender suddenly made intuitive sense to many students. Likewise, when we watched Cheryl Dunye's film *The Watermelon Woman*, students drew connections to Alison's examination of a queer archive to inform her relationships and developing construction of self with Cheryl's recovery of a racially-coded, cinematic archive for similar purposes. Again, multiple readings, students saw, were necessary to find— or create, as it were—a sense of one's place in history and a greater sense of one's identity.

Daily Life Performance

As students in this class improved at applying challenging theoretical ideas to *Fun Home*, they also began to apply these theories to their lived experiences. Reading and rereading, which is in itself rehearsed behavior, prompts Alison to become aware of how social institutions define and place limits on possible behavioral performances. For example, when Alison expresses that she doesn't care "if the necklines" of her dress and undershirt match, her father requires her to change clothing (Bechdel 15). Alison must wear feminine attire, deemed appropriate by her father (and, likely by extension, society), despite her preference for wear mismatching necklines or less traditionally feminine attire altogether. The behavior she is required to perform does not support how she identifies in the world. Thus, as Alison reads and rereads various sources, her gender performance becomes more subversive of the existing norms to which she was required to conform as a child. Because of her developing awareness, Alison eventually refuses to perform in accord with her father's gendered expectations. Her journey illuminates how our own behaviors incorporate the external and internal pressures placed upon us to act in a particular manner and can help students recognize the ways in which we might intentionally or unintentionally reify social norms by rehearsing the behaviors commonly associated with them.

Anecdotes from students suggest that, like Alison, their reading and rereading of *Fun Home* led to their questioning of normative social expectations and, on occasion, their embracing of unexplored components of their own identities. For instance, in one of our classes, an exercise science major questioned why male and female athletes had different protocols for spotting and weight-lifting in their training regimens. Another student examined the gendered rhetoric behind the national "Little Black Dress" campaign and critiqued the posters used to advertise this campaign as based, in part, on assumptions that reinforced gendered stereotypes. In one class, despite little prior experience with women's or gender studies, students' final papers focused on complex topics ranging from radical queer critiques of consumerism, representations of Westernized identity in *Persepolis*, homosocial norms in *The Illiad*, the neuroscience of transgender phenomena, debates about Beyoncé's brand of third-wave feminism, and the erasure of historical context in the camp musical *Victor/Victoria*. In short, students readily brought their new-found knowledge to bear on their professional and personal interests. Several years later, students still remark on how revelatory *Fun Home* was as they formed their own emerging identities and values near the start of their college careers.

What is clear from these examples is that the textual and intertextual performances of Bechdel's graphic novel influence students' understandings of the ways various texts (including behavior) work together to generate shifting meanings. Furthermore, in a pedagogical theatre, we explore the ways these meanings collide with and support social expectations and norms, and interrogate how our own rehearsed behaviors support and/or subvert these expectations. The layers of intertextuality in the classroom and in daily behaviors move beyond the narrative of the text we study and co-mingle in a single space, which David Osbon suggests might be explored as "transmedia intertextuality" (21). Relying on Marsha Kinder and Henry Jenkins, Osbon asserts that transmedia intertextuality occurs when a "particular narrative is presented across a range of [media] formats with different levels of interaction" to create "a potential performance environment in which an audience member can assemble their own interpretation of the narrative from the range of platforms and genres to which they have access" (21). Though Osbon goes on to discuss a particular multimedia artistic performance, we can apply this definition of transmedia intertextuality to our pedagogical theatre wherein the layers of performance occur in a wide variety of mediums that eventually come together. In particular, studying and learning to deconstruct these different levels of meaning, especially as they are presented within a graphic novel, may enhance students' developing understandings of intertextual performances. Furthermore, this continual process of connecting their analysis of a particular text and then synthesizing that text across another text or into their lived experiences can help students to better understand the complex constructions that undergird the world in which they live.

Graphic Novels and Pedagogical Theatre

Despite common misperceptions, comics and graphic novels are not an inherently "easy" medium, but rather a complex one that demands simultaneous engagement with several modalities and reading strategies. Nonetheless, many students find graphic texts approachable. This approachability may help instructors to more safely introduce students to queer and intersectional identities, which are topics that many of our students have not had the opportunity to consider, much less to discuss in a public setting. As Aimee Vincent states:

> Comics are in some ways the best kind of text available for such a potentially difficult discussion [about queer identities]. While I strongly oppose the concept that comics are an "easy" text to read, there is still popular perception that they are easy. When introducing a concept that has the potential to be difficult even for engaged and respectful students, a non-threatening medium like comics may diffuse some of the tension. (113–114)

The perception among many students that comics are "easy" results in fewer students erecting barriers to engaging with the ostensible content when comic readings are assigned, which potentially translates into students erecting fewer barriers as they learn to think through the ideologically challenging concepts of sexuality and queer identities. With a college-aged protagonist, *Fun Home* offers a text that students generally find compelling due to the immediacy of its imagery and its relatable plot. We find that we can use this general interest to help beginning college students carefully decode the graphic memoir's intricate motifs. Indeed, graphic novels and comics help students see how a text, which at first glance may seem simple and straightforward, can reveal a bewildering array of complexity. In teaching comics, we scaffold increasingly sophisticated reading practices and encourage students to read and reread with these different scaffolded layers in mind. Furthermore, in *Fun Home*, the medium discloses the underlying complexity of gender and sexual identities, a topic too many students initially view as straightforward, but that requires an array of interpretive and critical skills to fully comprehend.

Fun Home offers students a model of a queer reader: Alison is someone who compellingly reinterprets canonical texts and actively seeks out neglected texts to supplement her learning. She brings personal experiences to her reading of literature and uses literature to illuminate her personal life. In doing so, she employs the power of figuration—both graphic and literary—as a means to comprehend and come to terms with changing relationships, sexual identities, and her own mortality. She thus resists conventionalized meanings and investigates different narrative and interpretive possibilities through means such as research, imagination, discussion, hypothesis testing, journaling, modeling, close reading, revision, and mapping. At one point, Alison rereads the same text as her father—a fashion spread of a male model with an open jacket—through a subversively queer lens that desires the butch accoutrement, though it should be noted her father's gaze is queer, too, as his gaze desires the model beneath the garb (Bechdel 100–101). The actual reader, who reads the book over *their* shoulders, is offered a "looking-glass" for seeing how one's critical perceptions can be shaped by different objects of desire within the same image, and the reader rabbit-holes down a mise en abyme of shifting and ever-multiplying diegetic levels. This example is one of many that shows how the processes of interpretation are never straightforward or easy for Alison; in fact, students—whether queer or not—can identify with Alison precisely because she foregrounds a confusing, anxiety-provoking, trial-and-error approach to engaging with texts and composing one's own as they, too, learn to understand and write about difficult literature.

Epilogue

In our practice as instructors teaching mostly first- and second-year college students, we find that, through helping our students understand the iterative processes of performing and audiencing, we can help them to better understand critical reading and writing processes as iterative. Moreover, seeing the classroom as a space for the rehearsal of not only academic skills, but also identity performance and socialization, affords us and our students an arena to test and explore new relationships and repertoires of behavior, as well as approaches to learning and engaging with the world. That such performances are fluid and fallible, at least in the context of the pedagogical theatre, allows students the freedom to question the norms, values, and institutions in which they partake. Students can then, hopefully, create their own pedagogical theatres as they incorporate their new-found performance repertoires into their daily lives and learning process.

The graphic memoir *Fun Home* has proven a particularly valuable text to introduce students to several interlinked concepts related to reading, writing, and performance. Most readers are able to embrace the medium of the graphic novel and, at least partly, identify with some of Alison's struggles.

More importantly, though, the text's own performances—of close reading, composition, and identity formation—model the reflexive processes required to hone one's critical reading and composition skills, whether the skill level be that of an early-career college student or seasoned professor. *Fun Home* acts to show how literature, art, and, by extension, the humanities play a vital role in developing self-understanding, social awareness, and a holistic approach to life beyond the classroom. Ultimately, our goal in teaching *Fun Home* is to generate learning practices within ourselves and our students that will extend beyond the classroom's pedagogical theatre and into the theatre of the greater world.

NOTES

1. Informed by prominent scholars since the 1960s, the term "performativity" and the practices related to it have shifted and grown tremendously. In this chapter, we intend the term to reflect the process of creating behavior and human practices that rely on an audience's response to one's own actions or a text. For further explication, see Austin (1962), Schechner (1985), and Butler (1988).
2. Throughout this chapter we use "Bechdel" to refer to the author of the graphic novel and "Alison" to refer to the character in the text.
3. In fact, mirrors are a pivotal material object within *Fun Home*, as is the concept of "mirroring," which is related to mimesis, a central notion of theatre and performance studies. To mirror another is to rehearse behavior by performing the behavior more than once. As we continue these rehearsals, the iterative behavior becomes embedded into our identity until we no longer think about the behavior and it becomes "second nature" and a part of who we are. Consider how children learn by watching others and adopting their words and mannerisms. In short, we are taught to perform beginning in infancy. The pioneering social psychologist Charles Horton Cooley (1922) terms this process the "looking-glass self." The many mirrors depicted in Bechdel's text reflect this process to the reader. Discussing the notion of "mirrors" with students and the roles mirrors play in the text often leads to incredibly fruitful and animated discussions.
4. Concept mapping depicts ideas students generate, written in bubbles, to show the relationships between each idea using arrows and a hierarchical arrangement, which creates a visual representation of the cognitive structure of students' reading practices. Theme webs use various themes from the text (often chosen by the instructor) as nodes in a circular diagram. Students are asked to physically draw connections between these thematic nodes and then justify the connecting line they drew. For example, each small group could be

assigned a different theme and given a different color marker to complete their part of the web of thematic connections.

5. Such as Susan Stryker's *Transgender History* or Judith Butler's "Performative Acts and Gender Constitution: An Essay in Phenomenology and Feminist Theory."

6. The concept of "as if" is a contemporary restating of Constantin Stanislavski's "magic if," which is a staple of contemporary acting technique in the US. For more information see *An Actor Prepares* (1936).

7. We focus on gender norms here because *Fun Home* is the foundational text to prompt these explorations. The activity is easily adaptable to other non-normative and socially visible identity positions.

Works Cited

Alexander, Bryant, et al., editors. *Performance Theories in Education: Power, Pedagogy, and the Politics of Identity*, Kindle ed., Routledge, 2005.

Austin, J.L. *How To Do Things with Words*. Harvard UP, 1962.

Cooley, Charles Horton. *Human Nature and the Social Order*, Revised ed. Scribner's Sons, 1922.

Bechdel, Alison. *Fun Home: A Family Tragicomic*. Mariner, 2006.

Butler, Judith. "Performative Acts and Gender Constitution: An Essay in Phenomenology and Feminist Theory." *Theatre Journal,* vol. 40, no. 4, Dec. 1988, pp. 519–531.

Osbon, David. "Transmedia Intertextuality—Does it Work in Performance: *Follow the Sun* as Proof of Concept Project." *International Journal of Music and Performing Arts*, vol. 4, no. 1, June 2016, pp. 21–24.

Stanislavski, Constantin. *An Actor Prepares*. Translated by Elizabeth Reynolds Hapgood, Reprint ed., Routledge, 1989.

Todd, Jason. "Interdisciplinarity Through Graphic Novels." *Phi Kappa Phi Forum,* Fall 2015, pp. 8–12.

Tucker, Bill. "The Flipped Classroom." *Education Next,* vol. 12, no.1, Winter 2012, pp. 82–83.

Vincent, Aimee. "Performativity in Comics: Representations of Gender and Sexuality in Alison Bechdel's *Fun Home*." Thesis, Colorado State University, 2011, *CSU Theses and Dissertations*. https://dspace.library.colostate.edu/handle/10217/48209?show=full

INDEX

Note: Page numbers followed by "n" refers to notes.

© The Author(s) 2018
A. Burger (ed.), *Teaching Graphic Novels in the English Classroom*,
DOI 10.1007/978-3-319-63459-3

Lightning Source UK Ltd.
Milton Keynes UK
UKHW020249241119
354110UK00011B/654/P